# WHAT DID YOU EXPECT?

*Part Two of
The Gabriels:
Election Year in the
Life of One Family*

*Richard Nelson*

**BROADWAY PLAY PUBLISHING INC**
224 E 62nd St, NY, NY 10065
www.broadwayplaypub.com
info@broadwayplaypub.com

WHAT DID YOU EXPECT?
© Copyright 2016 by Richard Nelson

Cover graphic compliments of The Public Theater

First printing: December 2016
I S B N: 978-0-88145-690-5

Book design: Marie Donovan
Typographic controls: Adobe InDesign
Typeface: Palatino
Printed and bound in the U S A

WHAT DID YOU EXPECT was first produced by
The Public Theater (Oskar Eustis, Artistic Director;
Patrick Willingham, Executive Director), opening on
16 September 2016. The cast and creative contributors
were:

MARY GABRIEL ..................................... Maryann Plunkett
PATRICIA GABRIEL ................................. Roberta Maxwell
GEORGE GABRIEL ............................................ Jay O Sanders
HANNAH GABRIEL ....................................... Lynn Hawley
JOYCE GABRIEL ................................................. Amy Warren
KARIN GABRIEL ................................................. Meg Gibson

Director ........................................................ Richard Nelson
Scenic designers ............................................. Susan Hilferty
                                                & Jason Ardizzone-West
Costume designer ........................................... Susan Hilferty
Lighting designer ........................................... Jennifer Tipton
Sound designers ...................... Scott Lehrer & Will Pickens
Production stage manager ........................ Theresa Flanagan
Stage manager ......................................... Jared Oberholtzer
Assistant director ............................................. Sash Bischoff
Production assistant ............................... Joseph Fernandez
Stage management intern .......................... Rebecca Schafer
Prop master .............................................. Claire M Kavanah

# CHARACTERS & SETTING

[*Thomas Gabriel, a novelist and playwright, died in November 2015, at the age of 64.*]

MARY GABRIEL, *61, Thomas' third wife, and widow, a retired doctor.*

PATRICIA GABRIEL, *82, Thomas' mother.*

GEORGE GABRIEL, *61, Thomas' brother, a piano teacher and cabinetmaker*

HANNAH GABRIEL, *fifties,* GEORGE'*s wife, and Thomas' sister-in-law, works for a caterer.*

JOYCE GABRIEL, *fifties, Thomas' sister, an associate costume designer.*

KARIN GABRIEL, *fifties, Thomas' first wife, an actress and now teacher.*

*The kitchen of the* GABRIEL'*s house, South Street, Rhinebeck, NY.*

*Time: Friday, September 16, 2016, 6:30 P M.*

*Note: In the published versions of The Gabriel plays, I use a single quotation mark to notate when the character is paraphrasing, and double quotation marks when the character is actually reading from a source.*

"You cease to suffer, you cease to hope."
**Harley Granville Barker**
from *The Secret Life*

For Maryann and Jay

# WHAT DID YOU EXPECT?

*(An empty room: the kitchen of the* GABRIELS' *house. South Street, Rhinebeck, New York.)*

*(Refrigerator, stove/oven [electric], sink; large wooden and rustic table used as a kitchen counter [with a drawer for silverware] is set beside another smaller table making an "L" shape; a bench with a back is to one side, facing the tables; a small desk; upstage a small cupboard. Chairs and a bench set upside down on the tables.)*

*(Exits: upstage to the unseen dining room; down left to the mudroom, back porch and back yard; down right leads to the rest of the house—living room [where there is a piano], the stairs to the bedrooms on the second floor, and to the front porch.)*

*(In the dark, Lucius'* Don't Just Sit There *plays through the main speakers.)*

*(*MARY, HANNAH, JOYCE *and* KARIN *enter with trays full of kitchen objects. They will create the 'life of the kitchen'.* GEORGE *enters, with plastic boxes of Thomas' papers; he sets some notebooks from the boxes on the bench and table, and the boxes themselves on the floor or on a chair.)*

*(As* JOYCE *and* GEORGE *leave, lights up and the music fades:)*

# 1.

## Boxes

*(Off, from the living room, someone plays the piano—with starts and stops—Faure's* Nocturne No. 1 [op. 33. No.1]. *This is a music lesson.)*

*(The timer ticks on the stove.)*

*(*HANNAH *sits, finishing cutting out cookies, using a drinking glass to cut out the round shapes of the cookie dough; she lays out the shaped dough on a cookie sheet.)*

*(*MARY *sits, peeling a potato over a cutting board.* KARIN, *notebook in hand, is in the midst of describing to* HANNAH *something she has read in this notebook:)*

KARIN: And the windows are lit up; so you can clearly see through.

HANNAH: It's night?

KARIN: It's night. You can't hear the people inside, of course; you can only see them. The family's inside. A child asleep against a woman—the mother. Thomas doesn't tell you that, but—. It's obvious, the mother. And a man: the father. And an old man. The whole family. And they seem—at peace.

MARY: *(To* HANNAH*)* Inside the house.

KARIN: Two men have come into the back garden. That's what the stage represents. The garden. They look back—at what we, the audience, see—through the lit-up windows: the family in their house. Someone's drumming his fingers on a table. The mother looks out—one of the men in the garden says to the other, "she's looking at us." But no, no, she can't see. She's looking out into the dark…I'm just summarizing.

HANNAH: Sure…

KARIN: 'What are we going to do?' asks one of the men. 'Should I try and get the father's attention? Get him to come outside and tell him that his young daughter's just drowned?" Then watching the family, he adds: *(She reads:)* "I have never seen a happier household." The other says, "No, no. Don't go to the window. It's best to tell them of it as simply as we can, as if a commonplace occurrence; and let's not appear too sad, or they'll feel that their sorrow must exceed ours, and they'll not know what to do… Let's knock on the side door, and go in as if nothing has happened. Come with me…"

*(Piano music continues off.)*

KARIN: The other man resists: *(Reads)* "Why do you want me to go too? I'm a stranger here. I was just passing by." "Because a misfortune announced by a single voice seems more definite and crushing. Alone, I'll have to say something right away; the moment I come in. Together, I can take my time, say something, how they found her… 'She was floating in the river; her hands clasped…' We can blur the pain in details." I don't know why but that moves me. 'Blur the pain in details…'

MARY: I've done that. As a doctor… With…details…

KARIN: *(Continues)* And the two men continue to talk like this: what to do, what can they do, while all the time—we, the audience, watch, through the window, the family go about their lives. It's an amazing play.

*(Timer soon goes off.)*

KARIN: Thomas has made a note to himself in the margins here: "Perhaps they make a meal? Have a dinner? Must feel normal… Make it normal…"

*(HANNAH will get up and take a cookie sheet of cookies out of the oven.)*

MARY: (*To* KARIN, *wiping her hands*) Where's that page where Thomas has circled everything in magic marker…?

(MARY *takes the notebook from* KARIN; HANNAH *will get a pot for the potatoes.*)

HANNAH: (*To* MARY) Had you read this play?

MARY: (*Shaking her head, looking through the notebook*) There were so many, Hannah… Here… One of the men says: (*Reads*) "They are awaiting the night, separated from us by only a few poor panes of glass. They think they are secure in their life, and do not dream that so many others know more of it than they…" And *this* is underlined: "And that I, a poor old man—" Thomas wrote in the margin, "that's me, that's me…" (*Looks at* HANNAH. *Continues*) "…a poor old man am two steps from their door, and hold all their little happiness, like a wounded bird, in the hollow of my old hands, and dare not open them…"

KARIN: (*Taking it back*) We stayed up most of last night reading this.

(HANNAH *looks at* MARY.)

MARY: (*To* HANNAH, *handing the notebook back*) We did…

KARIN: (*As she looks for the page*) And one of the old men, who's watching the family, says to the other— that he'd seen their daughter -

MARY: The dead daughter.

KARIN: —just this morning. She'd told him she was going to see a friend on the other side of the river. (*Listing:*) How beautiful she was. Her lovely hair… (*Turns page*) Here: "the daughter was just living this morning!" (*The list:*) What she might have become. All the friends she had. While inside the house now, they're smiling. Someone's playing the piano. (*She*

*notices the coincidence—someone is playing the piano here.
And gestures.)*

MARY: *(To* HANNAH*)* Playing the piano...

(HANNAH *nods.)*

KARIN: Someone inside has said something funny...

HANNAH: So then what happens?

MARY: Before the old men get up the courage to tell
the family, some people from the town bring the body
to the house; and so—the family learns. While still
outside, the two men and—

KARIN: —and of course, we, the audience—

MARY: —just *see* this, through the lit window, without
*hearing* anything. We just watch—everything going on
inside.

KARIN: Finally one of the old men watching all this,
says, *(Turns a few pages)* —and this is the last line of the
play... *(Reads)* "Look." He says, "Look. Their baby is
still asleep." The title is "Interior".

HANNAH: I didn't know Thomas even did
translations...

MARY: He did...

HANNAH: He didn't know any languages, did he?

MARY: He worked with friends. *(About the potatoes, over
the noise of the water, to* HANNAH*)* These enough?

HANNAH: I don't need more than five.... *(She goes to the
sink to fill a pot for the potatoes with water.)*

MARY: I peeled too many then. I got carried away. We
can have them tonight then with the sausages... Cook
them together. I just kept peeling... *(Smiles)*

HANNAH: *(Wiping her hands)* May I see?

KARIN: *(Handing her the notebook)* From the French...

HANNAH: I was never any good at languages…

MARY: Something he got really interested in doing, right before getting sick. I think he and his friends had plans to do a lot more… *(She will go and throw out the peelings.)*

HANNAH: Translations?

MARY: *(Pointing to a page with names, to* HANNAH*)* Those are his friends. Those two. They're the real translators, he always said. They'd done novels. *(About the potatoes)* You wanted them cut small, right? It's potato salad…

HANNAH: *(Handing back the notebook to* KARIN*, to* MARY*)* Whatever. Doesn't matter…

KARIN: *(About the notebook)* He puts a different picture on each notebook—

MARY: Cut up postcards—

KARIN: Postcards.

HANNAH: What's that one of?

KARIN: A house. Just a house…

MARY: *(As she cuts)* One day the three of them—

*(As* HANNAH *fills the pot with water from the sink:)*

MARY: The three of them—Thomas and his translator friends—are sitting in the friends' kitchen, working on their first translation together. They worked in the kitchen. *(To* KARIN*)* I told you this… *(To* HANNAH*)* And they'd been at it for a couple of days, when one of his friends says. "Thomas, we've been translating for much of our lives—"

*(*HANNAH *will take the pot, set it on the stove. About the potatoes to* HANNAH*:)*

MARY: This okay?

*(*HANNAH *nods.)*

MARY: "And" the friend says, "You just keep asking us one question that we never ever ask ourselves, when translating novels."

HANNAH: What's the question?

KARIN: 'Why?'

MARY: 'Why?'

HANNAH: 'Why' what?

MARY: *(About KARIN)* She asked that too. Thomas said he had to explain to his friends that with a play unlike a novel, where you're just trying to get the right words, with a play, what you are really trying to translate are the author's people.

HANNAH: I'm not sure I understand.

KARIN: The characters.

HANNAH: I understood that.

MARY: And so that's why, he said, he was always asking his friends: 'why does he say what he says or she says, and why now, and why him and not her, and so forth.' To translate the people.

*(HANNAH will take a bowl of the cut potatoes and pour the cut and peeled potatoes into the water on the stove and turn on the burner.)*

MARY: Interesting…I should probably start our dinner…

HANNAH: *(To KARIN)* Is that what you tell your Hotchkiss kids?

KARIN: God only knows what they hear… *(As a joke)* God only knows what I tell them. Whatever the hell comes out.

MARY: Hannah, I remembered something else last night with Karin… *(She gathers ingredients for the casserole dish.)*

KARIN: What?

MARY: That actor—what he said by... *(Mistake)*?

KARIN: *(To* HANNAH*)* Oh this is funny.

HANNAH: What?

MARY: The first play of his that Thomas ever took me to see... We'd just met. I think it might even have been the first performance. Hannah, there was a scene where an Uncle had to kill his nephew, what was the name, the nephew had a funny name?

KARIN: Doesn't matter.

MARY: It doesn't matter. To kill his nephew in order, he said, to save—face? *(Shrugs)* I don't remember why. To save face. Anyway, the actor playing the Uncle— *(To* KARIN*)* Thomas used to play squash with him, I just remembered that. *(Continues)* The actor, the Uncle, was supposed to say; I have to get this right. Supposed to say: "Come, Nephew, sit and let me save your face."

KARIN: *(To* HANNAH*)* That's what he's supposed to say.

HANNAH: Okay.

MARY: "Come, Nephew, sit and let me save your face." But instead of this, the actor, the Uncle, said, and said it really really loud: said, "Come Nephew, and let me sit on your face..."

*(Laughter)*

*(To* HANNAH*)* All the other actors on the stage, they turned their backs to the audience, and you just saw their shoulders going up and down...I didn't notice. Thomas told me later...

KARIN: *(Closing a box)* I've looked through everything in this one, Mary. Want me to get another?

MARY: A couple more if you can carry them...

(KARIN *gets up and starts to go off to the office with the box.*)

HANNAH: How late were you two up last night?

KARIN: *(As she goes)* It was her birthday…

MARY: Not everyone goes to bed at ten, Hannah.

HANNAH: I don't always go to bed at—.

MARY: It was my birthday.

(KARIN *is gone.*)

MARY: *(Back to the story)* The theater, Hannah…! I don't know how the actors learn their lines. And it must get really hard as they get older…

HANNAH: You're all right with her…?

MARY: Here? She's paying rent.

HANNAH: *(Beginning a list)* Going through all of Thomas' stuff…

MARY: It's not 'stuff.' And there's plenty of room. And I asked her. She wasn't looking to stay. She was going to rent the place she had last time. And she knows theater. That's a big help.

*(Off, the phone is ringing)*

MARY: *(Again, standing)* She's paying rent…

HANNAH: Let George—

MARY: He's giving a lesson.

*(Piano stops.)*

HANNAH: He's getting it.

MARY: I remembered something else last night, talking with Karin.

*(Phone stops ringing.)*

MARY: Once Thomas was so pleased… He'd come across a listing of titles of 'lost plays' —just the titles,

the plays didn't exist anymore, by some old Irish writer
from the 19th century. Somehow they knew the titles—

HANNAH: *(Explaining)* Probably some academic
compiled—.

MARY: I suppose. And he reads me one title, and says,
*(Imitates Thomas)* 'Oh I could make a play from this.'

*(HANNAH smiles at the imitation. She has been gathering
ingredients for her potato salad.)*

MARY: You know how he loved obscure stuff. That no
one else knew about. He was so competitive.

HANNAH: He was a Gabriel.

MARY: He even starts to write it. You want to know
what that title was? *"Shakespeare in Love."*

HANNAH: And then the movie comes out. I never heard
this.

MARY: *(Over this)* And he's really pissed off. *(As
Thomas)* 'That's my fucking play.' Actually, I tell him,
it was this dead Irish guy's play. He says he's going
to write it anyway. Who the hell is going to see this
stupid movie? We go to Upstate to see it...

HANNAH: That's where George and I saw it.

MARY: *(Over this)* It's been playing like four weeks, and
we can still hardly get in...

HANNAH: *(Same time)* We loved it.

MARY: We can't even sit together. *(Remembering)* You
said you wanted to see my Moosewood potato salad
recipe.

HANNAH: Never mind. I really do not care whether
they like it or not...

*(HANNAH at the refrigerator takes out mustard.)*

MARY: I doubt if that's true. You still have your pride...
I'm going to need the mustard too...

HANNAH: Do I still have my pride? Are we so sure? *(Sets herself up to make potato salad.)*

MARY: *(Another story)* Once we were at the Book Barn in Hillsdale.

HANNAH: You and Thomas?

MARY: And Thomas has—. I didn't tell Karin this. I just remembered this this morning. *(Continues)* Thomas has a book open and he shows me an inscription written inside. 'To Helen' or someone, I forget, 'You deserve to have a whole chapter devoted just to you.'

HANNAH: Sweet…

MARY: Guess what the title was? *Bitch.* Some novel…

HANNAH: Did he buy the book? Thomas?

MARY: I don't remember. He didn't buy it for me.

HANNAH: This all the balsamic you have?

MARY: You need more?

HANNAH: *(Looks at it)* It should be fine. Onion?

*(MARY hands HANNAH an onion as:)*

HANNAH: So Karin is comfortable in the office?

MARY: Upstairs. No complaints.

HANNAH: She's only been there a couple of days, Mary.

MARY: Hannah—

HANNAH: I'm not sure I'd want my husband's ex-wife—

MARY: I didn't know George had an ex-wife.

HANNAH: You know what I mean. Digging through his old things—.

MARY: I don't think she's '*digging*'.

HANNAH: *Dragging* up then—.

MARY: I asked for her help…. And it doesn't need to be 'dragged up'. It's already there. *(Then, again)* She knows theater. She's an actress. I'm fine. *(She has begun to organize a sausage casserole.)*

HANNAH: It was probably Joyce on the phone.

MARY: Probably. *(Another memory)* Once Thomas and I were visiting Patricia. This is about almost—twenty years ago—when we first got married? And we drive out to that little shopping plaza on Route 9.

HANNAH: Across from the fairgrounds—?

MARY: *(Over the end of this)* To that wine store. I don't know why he wanted to go to that wine store…
But there's a mostly comics bookshop there too. It's gone now. But they also had a few used books along with the comics. Thomas *has* to go. I wait outside…
*(Dramatic pause)*

HANNAH: What???

MARY: He comes out with that huge stupid grin on his face.

HANNAH: I remember that grin.

MARY: *(Over this)* He's got a book under his arm. 'Let's get in the car. Let's go. Let's go.' Then we stop in front of the Fairgrounds; and he shows me the book…
Beautiful jacket. Perfect condition. Thomas explains, 'it was only the first printing that he allowed his photo on the jacket.'

HANNAH: Who?

MARY: The author. That's why it's worth so much. You don't know this?

HANNAH: No.

MARY: This was way before we moved here… He paid like four dollars and seventy-five cents for this book. He said he even felt bad cheating the guy in the store.

He kept it in a baggie in a bookcase for about five years, then sold it to a dealer in New York. Paid for a trip to Europe…. *The Catcher in the Rye…* We could use that money now.

(HANNAH *and* MARY *see* GEORGE *entering:*)

MARY: We should have kept it.

GEORGE: What should we have kept? What the hell have we thrown away now?

MARY: Nothing, George.

HANNAH: Was that your sister on the phone?

GEORGE: She's picked up Mom. They'll be here in a minute.

HANNAH: How long has Joyce been there?

GEORGE: I don't know. I didn't ask… We're almost done. *(Starts to head off)*

HANNAH: Did Danny bring a check?

GEORGE: He forgot… *(He goes off.)*

HANNAH: *(Calls)* Remind him to ask his mother… Do you want me to call her? And it's been more than an hour…! He always goes over—.

MARY: Not always—.

HANNAH: And he leaves time between. Because he never wants to keep anyone *waiting*. I tell him *no one* does that. No one. Only George does that. His lessons are supposed to be for one hour…

(KARIN *enters with two boxes. She will set them down near the bench.*)

MARY: Joyce called. They'll be here in a minute.

KARIN: There's a full moon…

MARY: Is there?

KARIN: Looks huge. *(About the boxes)* There must be twenty, thirty notebooks in this one… And files…

HANNAH: *(To* MARY*)* How many boxes are left?

MARY: *(Shrugs)* I don't know…

HANNAH: Mary was just telling me, Karin, what a help you are. Because you know the names. You know theater…

*(Lights fade.)*

## 2.
## Arrivals

*(A short time later. The same.)*

*(The piano lesson continues in the living room.)*

*(When the water boils in the pot of potatoes,* HANNAH *will turn down the burner, and occasionally poke the potatoes. In the meantime, she continues to prepare the other ingredients in a bowl.)*

*(*MARY*, with a notebook from the new box, is in the middle of explaining an entry:)*

MARY: He didn't want to be there. Thomas could always make that clear.

KARIN: Oh, yes, he could. He could.

MARY: This time I stick to my guns. I'd taken a course in Greek art in college, so I thought it'd be interesting. And after all I had sat through a *four-and-a-half hour* fucking play—in *German.* So… I figured he owed me this. *(She looks back at the notebook.)*

KARIN: I agree.

MARY: 'Go ahead and mope, Thomas… Go ahead… But you're coming with me to this goddamn museum.'

HANNAH: Fair is fair.

KARIN: *When* were you in Berlin?

MARY: *(To* HANNAH*)* Maybe—twelve, thirteen years ago?

HANNAH: Don't ask me.

KARIN: *(As a 'joke')* Thomas never took me anywhere… *(She is taking out another notebook.)*

MARY: *(Over the end of this, to* HANNAH*)* I'm looking into a glass cabinet—at papyrus fragments. You push a button and a tray moves… *(Demonstrates)* Some of my college education is coming back. Then—I see a label: *'theater.'* I push this button labeled— *'theater.'* 'Thomas,' I say, 'Thomas!'*(Gestures for him to come to her)* He grudgingly comes over to the cabinet, just as this papyrus slowly, very slowly comes into view. They had a description in German and in English. *(Looks at the notebook)* "The only existing fragment of this play which is by —Euripides." *(Thomas' voice)* 'Mary, by Euripides!' My god, I'd found something that interested him! You don't know how hard that was to do… *(To* KARIN*)* It was probably easier for you, being an actress…

KARIN: *(A 'joke')* Obviously it wasn't.

MARY: *(She 'laughs'; hands the notebook to* HANNAH*)* Here… There, read that.

HANNAH: *(Wipes hands, takes the notebook)* That's funny. *(Reads)* "I am a woman, but I have — intelligence…"

*(Front doorbell off.)*

HANNAH: *(To* MARY*)* They're here. *(Reads)* "I am a woman, but I have—intelligence…" It's the 'but'…

MARY: I know.

*(Two or three impatient doorbells)*

HANNAH: *(Obviously, to* MARY*)* Joyce.

*(The piano music stops.)*

MARY: There was just this papyrus fragment… That's
all that's left of this play. I remember Thomas writing
all this down. He was excited; 'Euripides, Mary!'
He said he could use it for something. I don't know
what…

*(KARIN has picked up another notebook.)*

MARY: *(Reads)* "In vain, it seems to me, do men mock
women; denigrate and speak badly of us. But the truth
is, women are better than men." 'Women are better
than men.' *(Reads)* "And—I shall prove it…" *That's*
where the papyrus is ripped off… The rest is lost…
"Women are better than men…"

*(GEORGE entering with a bottle of wine:)*

GEORGE: Joyce is in the bathroom.

MARY: Did you hear that, George?

GEORGE: Hear what?

MARY: "Women are better than—"?

HANNAH: *(Over this)* Never mind. What's that?

GEORGE: *(Holds up bottle)* Joyce… Probably stole it from
her boss's party. *(Looking at the label)* It's nice wine…

HANNAH: How is Joyce?

GEORGE: *(Over this)* Screw top. That used to mean…

KARIN: It used to.

*(GEORGE puts the wine in the refrigerator.)*

GEORGE: *(Over this)* It'll be nice to have a change.
Something decent.

HANNAH: *(Again)* Joyce okay?

GEORGE: She had to use the bathroom. I don't know…

HANNAH: And your mother?

(GEORGE *Is gone. The timer goes off.*)

MARY: *(To* HANNAH*)* You need help?

HANNAH: No.

MARY: It's good Joyce is here. She should be. *(To* HANNAH, *about the timer)* Your cookies...

HANNAH: I know. *(She will go to take her cookies out of the oven, and will slowly, with a spatula, separate the cookies from the sheet as:)*

KARIN: *(With the other notebook, to say something) This* is interesting. The phrase or whatever it is— 'O K'? The phrase— 'O K'?

HANNAH: *(Obviously)* We know the phrase 'O K'.

KARIN: *(Referring to the notebook)* It comes from 'Old Kinderhook', the Van Buren campaign for President... Thomas wrote that down for some reason... Everyone uses 'O K', all around the world.

MARY: *(To* HANNAH*)* Kinderhook's just up the road.

HANNAH: Not that close.

KARIN: *(Another entry)* Here's something else. 'George Frederic Jones.'

MARY: *(To* HANNAH*)* Joyce is going to want coffee...I'll heat it up. Who's that, Karin?

HANNAH: *(About the coffee)* How long has that been sitting there?

MARY: *(Looking into the coffee pot)* I don't know.

KARIN: *(Skimming the notebook)* This Jones seems to have had a house in Rhinebeck, near Wilderstein... And, I think what Thomas is saying is, this is where the phrase 'keeping up with the Joneses' comes from. Huh. *(Amazed) Rhinebeck!* This whole notebook seems to be about Rhinebeck.

MARY: *(Seeing Joyce coming, to* HANNAH*)* Joyce...

KARIN: *(Reading in the notebook)* 'Rufus Wainwright was born in Rhinebeck…'

MARY: *(Greeting)* Joyce… *(Wiping her hands)* My hands are wet… Let me… *(Keeps wiping them)*

JOYCE: *(Over this)* Hannah…

HANNAH: *(Working her cookies, over this)* I'll give you a hug in a minute, Joyce.

MARY: *(Going to give JOYCE a hug)* Karin's here…

JOYCE: I know. Nice to see you again, Karin.

KARIN: Back like a bad penny…

HANNAH: Don't say that.

MARY: Hannah, she's joking.

JOYCE: Here are Mom's car keys… Why haven't we sold that car? *(Sets keys on the table.)*

MARY: When the sticker runs out.

HANNAH: *(Same time)* It's worth like nothing. *(Going to give Joyce a hug)* Nice top.

JOYCE: Thrift store. I got lucky.

HANNAH: *(Getting up)* Where's Patricia?

JOYCE: Oh she's coming…I behaved.

HANNAH: *(Hugging JOYCE)* Really good to see you…

JOYCE: You too.

MARY: *(Putting the keys in the desk, to say something)* Karin's rented the guest room above the office.

JOYCE: George told me. I always found up there spooky at night, Karin.

HANNAH: Me too.

MARY: Don't tell her that.

KARIN: *(To HANNAH)* Why is it spooky?

MARY: Nothing, Karin. *(To* JOYCE*)* I'll heat up the coffee.

JOYCE: Thanks. Any tea? I'm drinking mostly tea now. Any Chai?

MARY: No. *(Looks to* HANNAH*)* No 'chai.' When have we ever had 'Chai' in this house, Joyce? How's Lipton? I think we have some Lipton… You'll settle for Lipton? *(Looks in the cabinet)*

JOYCE: Anything's fine. I brought wine. George grabbed it from me.

HANNAH: *(Over this, about the wine)* In the refrigerator. It's 'waiting'…

JOYCE: *(As she checks)* My boss bought cases and cases. But rich Democrats now don't drink that much anymore. They seem to be mostly young guys watching their weight.

*(Seeing* GEORGE *entering:)*

HANNAH: Where's your mother?

GEORGE: *(Entering)* Taking off her jacket. Very slowly. Just one more practice piece, Hannah, okay?

HANNAH: George…

GEORGE: *(Over this)* Danny's been working hard. He's earned it. Listen…

*(Off, Danny has been playing musical scales.)*

GEORGE: *(Incredulous)* On his own… *(He goes.)*

HANNAH: *(Calls)* Tell him to ask his mother about the check… *(To* JOYCE*)* Danny's Mom owes us a check. Your brother keeps forgetting to ask…

JOYCE: Sounds like my brother.

MARY: I'll heat your water.

JOYCE: I can do that, Mary. Let me do that. *(To* HANNAH*)* What are you doing? What is all this?

MARY: *(Explaining)* Hannah's making stuff for a picnic tomorrow. If it doesn't rain.

HANNAH: *(Quoting* GEORGE*)* "Even if it rains…"

MARY: *(A list)* The cookies…

JOYCE: *(Over this)* A picnic. I can't remember the last time I went on a picnic. Watch out for ticks. *(To* MARY*)* Any mug?

MARY: Doesn't matter.

*(*JOYCE *takes a mug from the dishrack. and begins to prepare her tea.)*

JOYCE: *(To* HANNAH*)* It's supposed to be nice tomorrow. Not crazy hot like last weekend. The city was unbearable. *(To* MARY*)* Is there honey?

MARY: On the stove. We keep it there now; so it doesn't get hard. I read that.

*(*PATRICIA *enters from the dining room:)*

PATRICIA: George is almost finished… Where do you want me to sit?

JOYCE: It's your kitchen, Mom.

HANNAH: Why don't you sit in your chair, Patricia. *(To* JOYCE*)* This has now become your mother's favorite chair.

JOYCE: Has it, Mom?

HANNAH: It's become that.

*(*MARY *goes to the cabinet, she will take out a couple of cans of beans, find a can opener in the drawer in the table, and open the two cans, as:)*

*(As* PATRICIA *sits:)*

JOYCE: George's student seems to be a very hard worker.

PATRICIA: Your brother is a wonderful teacher, Joyce.

JOYCE: I know he is. He taught me.

HANNAH: Mary's making your famous sausage casserole… How often do we have Joyce to dinner?

PATRICIA: Not very often.

JOYCE: I come when I can, Mom. *(To* HANNAH*)* I left my boss' car at Mom's 'inn'. It's safe there?

HANNAH: Why wouldn't it be safe? *(To* PATRICIA*)* I'm glad you're feeling better.

JOYCE: You weren't feeling well, Mom? You didn't say…

HANNAH: This morning your mother said she had a headache.

PATRICIA: I did have a headache… *(She smiles at* KARIN.*)*

JOYCE: That's Karin, Mom, she's—

PATRICIA: I know Karin. I know who she is. Hello, Karin.

KARIN: Hi—Pat.

JOYCE: 'Pat'??

HANNAH: Your mother 'remembered' yesterday—she says, Karin used to call her 'Pat.'

PATRICIA: I just remembered.

JOYCE: Dad called you that.

MARY: *(To* PATRICIA*)* You want tea? Now we're making tea. We're branching out.

PATRICIA: No, thank you, Mary.

JOYCE: *(Smelling the Lipton)* I don't need tea. Coffee's fine… *(She will pour herself some coffee.)*

KARIN: Mary…?

MARY: Wait for George. Then you can work in the living room. It's comfortable in there.

HANNAH: *(To* JOYCE, *to say something)* We all went out last night to that new Indian for Mary's birthday. Your mother too.

JOYCE: I'm sorry I missed your birthday.

MARY: It was a birthday…

JOYCE: So there's a new Indian in the village?

HANNAH: It's not cheap.

JOYCE: It's Rhinebeck. What did you expect? Why did you go to the Indian?

MARY: It's new. We hadn't been.

HANNAH: Mary wanted to go somewhere she hadn't been with Thomas. It just opened in January. You want another pillow, Patricia? Let me get you a pillow…

*(As they watch* MARY *pour in the beans into the casserole:)*

PATRICIA: I always made this meal on *Sunday* nights, Mary.

MARY: So did I, Patricia. For Thomas.

*(*HANNAH *puts a pillow behind* PATRICIA*:)*

HANNAH: Is that better…?

PATRICIA: *(To* HANNAH*)* You're a dear.

JOYCE: *(With her coffee, the notebooks)* So what's all this stuff, Mary?

HANNAH: Joyce, it's not 'stuff.'

MARY: *(Explains:)* We're going through Thomas' old notebooks… Seeing what, if anything, we can sell…

*(Lights fade.)*

## 3.
## Mom's 'Inn'

*(The same. A little while later)*

*(Off, piano music. The lesson continues; still the Faure.)*

*(HANNAH and MARY continue their preparations [for the potato salad and casserole, respectively; with MARY cutting up onions and the sausages]. KARIN listens to JOYCE, and continues to look through the notebooks and boxes.)*

*(PATRICIA sits and listens.)*

*(JOYCE in the middle of conversation, as she sips her coffee:)*

KARIN: Did you get to shake Bill Clinton's hand?

JOYCE: He was there for like five minutes. I never even got near him.

MARY: He's had a very busy week—.

HANNAH: —filling in. Mary, why won't she drink water?

MARY: I don't know. I'm not her doctor.

HANNAH: Any coffee, Patricia?

JOYCE: You want some, Mom?

*(PATRICIA shakes her head.)*

JOYCE: They say she's all better now.

HANNAH: In one week? From pneumonia? Mary?

MARY: I'm not her doctor.

KARIN: I have a friend, a reporter. He was at a reception with the Clintons? In D C, I think. And he took his wife. And she told me that when he talked to her? Bill. You know it's famous how— 'you're-the-

only-person-in-the-room' when he talks to you? She
found that really creepy.

JOYCE: We're not blaming her for that.

HANNAH: What do you need, Patricia?

JOYCE: She doesn't need to be waited on.

PATRICIA: No, Joyce, I don't. Thank you, Hannah. I
don't need anything.

KARIN: If I met him, I don't know what I'd say to him.

JOYCE: Met who, Karin??

KARIN: *(Obviously)* Bill Clinton.

MARY: He's done a lot of good too, hasn't he? I
remember him doing good.

KARIN: He always sounds so damn convincing. And I
always end up so damn 'convinced'...

JOYCE: How can I help? Let me do something.

MARY: Hannah?

HANNAH: Chop up the parsley...?

JOYCE: Sure. I'll do that. I can do that.

MARY: *(Over this)* Joyce, why do you have to go back
tonight—?

PATRICIA: You're going back tonight?

JOYCE: You know that, Mom. I told you.

(HANNAH *will get the parsley and a cutting board for*
JOYCE.)

JOYCE: Tomorrow's the *millionaires*—for brunch. Last
night it was the *billionaires*—and their friends. We
think my boss wants to be ambassador to—something.
Somewhere where people dress really really well.
And change their clothes a lot. Gillibrand's coming
tomorrow. That's the rumor.

HANNAH: I'll bet she's a lot of fun. *(To* JOYCE*)* That needs to be washed. I'll need about a cup. *(Of parsley)*

*(Off the piano music has stopped.)*

HANNAH: I think he's done. *(Looks at her watch)*

*(*JOYCE *will go to wash the parsley in the sink.)*

HANNAH: Patricia, did George tell you we already got a nibble on the piano?

*(*PATRICIA *nods.)*

JOYCE: Did we?

HANNAH: *(To* JOYCE*)* Someone from Bard. A singer. So we had it tuned this morning.

JOYCE: If you had to. *(Then back to the party:)* My boss loaned all us assistants these amazing dresses.

KARIN: What do you mean? What dresses?

HANNAH: She wanted you to look rich. To fit in.

PATRICIA: What was yours, Joyce? Was it very nice? I'd like to see you in a nice dress.

JOYCE: I wear dresses, Mom. *(To* HANNAH*)* Sort of Fifties. Big pattern of flowers. Summery.

MARY: Probably something like you once wore, Patricia.

HANNAH: *(To* PATRICIA*)* And I'll bet you looked great in it too.

PATRICIA: I think I did.

KARIN: I'm sure you did, Pat.

JOYCE: Perfect neck for me. Squared. Thick straps. She knows... Perfect weight. It moved, you know, when you walked, I felt great...

HANNAH: You want something to do, Patricia?

*(*PATRICIA *shakes her head.)*

KARIN: Was there any dancing?

JOYCE: *(Of course not)* No. *(Back at the table to chop the parsley.)*

PATRICIA: Joyce doesn't dance, Karin.

JOYCE: I dance, Mom. I dance. Why do you say that?

PATRICIA: I thought you hated dancing.

JOYCE: I hated ballet class, Mom. When I was like eight years old.

PATRICIA: *(Her point proved)* That's what I remember.

JOYCE: Jesus…I dance.

PATRICIA: I didn't know that.

JOYCE: My boss had sandals for us too. Waiting in our closets. I looked mine up on line. Guess how much, Mom?

PATRICIA: I have no idea, Joyce.

JOYCE: Over a thousand dollars, Mom. *(To the others)* For a couple of thin pieces of leather strips sewn together…

HANNAH: For shoes? Who are these people?

JOYCE: They weren't even comfortable.

*(JOYCE sees GEORGE entering.)*

JOYCE: There you are. Here he is.

HANNAH: Finished?

GEORGE: Danny will ask his mother for a check… He's been working so hard…

MARY: Good for Danny…

HANNAH: *(To GEORGE)* Joyce has been telling us about her boss's fundraiser for Hillary in Hudson.

MARY: For very very rich people.

GEORGE: *(Getting out the water pitcher from the refrigerator)* I'm sorry I couldn't make it. I hope they understood. Anyone else want water?

*(They don't.)*

MARY: *(To* GEORGE*)* Joyce has to go back after dinner. She can't stay the night.

GEORGE: I figured.

PATRICIA: *(To* JOYCE*)* You sure you can't stay—?

JOYCE: No, Mom.

MARY: She has another fundraiser tomorrow. Gillibrand might be there.

GEORGE: What does she need money for?

JOYCE: *(Starting a list)* For Teachout...

GEORGE: No. God, please no...

*(As* KARIN *looks at* MARY *and starts to get up:)*

KARIN: Mary...

MARY: Thank you, Karin. We won't be too long.

KARIN: *(Over the end of this)* Of course. *(As she picks up a box)* Maybe I'll find a treasure...

MARY: Thank you.

HANNAH & JOYCE: Thanks.

PATRICIA: Thank you, Karin.

*(*KARIN *is gone.)*

JOYCE: *(To* PATRICIA*)* She lives here now...

PATRICIA: I know, Joyce.

MARY: Dinner's not for an hour.

JOYCE: You look good, Mom.

GEORGE: Doesn't she.

HANNAH: *(To* JOYCE*)* What did you think of your
Mother's new room?

JOYCE: *(Turns to* PATRICIA*)* I really liked it, Mom.
It's not as crowded as I thought it would feel with a
roommate. It's cozy.

HANNAH: *(To* PATRICIA*)* Was the roommate there?

*(*PATRICIA *nods.)*

JOYCE: You didn't even know her before, did you,
Mom?

PATRICIA: No.

JOYCE: I hadn't known that… *(Then)* So—Mom, what
do you pay now? How much a month? I think I need to
start there….

*(*PATRICIA *looks to* GEORGE.*)*

GEORGE: It's now forty-five hundred a month, Mom.

PATRICIA: It had been more for a single.

GEORGE: It was. And that was a big help. *(To* JOYCE*)*
Her moving herself into the double room cut about a
thousand-plus off a month.

HANNAH: *(To* PATRICIA*)* You did that yourself. *(To*
JOYCE*)* You lied and told us you 'wanted company…'

JOYCE: *(To* PATRICIA*)* So what exactly do you owe them,
Mom?

HANNAH: *(Trying to be light)* Joyce, this young guy
stopped Mary the other day, when she was visiting
your Mother. He said, "Mrs Gabriel, your mother-in-
law has no more than a month left." Mary thought—.

MARY: Of course I thought…

JOYCE: He was from the business office.

HANNAH: You'd think he'd find a different way of
putting it.

JOYCE: He said the exact same thing to me. Just now.
The moment I walked into Mom's room, he came in.
And he knew who I was.

MARY: You signed in. They call back to the office when
any of us signs in now…

GEORGE: Mom, you owe two months, and now this
month. That's about thirteen thousand and change. To
get you through the rest of September.

JOYCE: The next two weeks…

GEORGE: Yeh.

*(Awkward pause)*

JOYCE: Do they kick people out? It's a 'home'. Do they
really do that?

GEORGE: It's a business, Joyce…

*(Then)*

JOYCE: This guy, Mom, from the office showed me
some of your bills. *(To the others)* Have you seen them?

HANNAH: *(Looking at GEORGE)* I think we have.

JOYCE: *(To PATRICIA)* 'Guest meals.' What is that, Mom?

MARY: *(Before PATRICIA can answer)* It's mostly us. *(To
PATRICIA)* You like us to come to dinner now and then,
don't you? *(To JOYCE)* We can stop doing that. That's
our fault.

JOYCE: *(The list)* 'Breakfast in the room'? He said, that's
not part of independent living—.

HANNAH: You pay extra for that.

MARY: Your mother got a terrible cold, Joyce.
Remember?

GEORGE: *(Over this)* We called you.

MARY: She didn't want to get dressed. It wasn't some
'luxurious' indulgence. Your Mom's not like that. *(To*

PATRICIA) You're not like that. *(To* JOYCE) You know that.

HANNAH: Your mother knows what she's done. And she's facing it. *(To* PATRICIA) Aren't you?

PATRICIA: I think so. I'm trying. *(To* JOYCE) What do you want to say?

*(Then)*

JOYCE: Remember telling me, Mom: 'we women, we have to be so damn tough'? *(Then)* Ever since George called, I've been hearing you say that to me. I remember you sitting me down in this very kitchen, here, and telling me 'to be careful, Joyce'. 'Watch out for yourself.' You never talked like that to Thomas or George.

PATRICIA: No. I didn't.

JOYCE: 'Joyce, we women must be responsible for ourselves.' 'We can't expect others to go around cleaning up our messes.' That used to get me so angry.

PATRICIA: I know. I'm sorry, Joyce.

*(Then:)*

JOYCE: What are you going to do, Mom?

HANNAH: We told your mother we're ready to dip into Paulie's college fund.

JOYCE: *(Shocked)* What? Are you serious? You can't do that. *(To* PATRICIA) You'd let them do that?

GEORGE: *(Over the end of this)* Some of it.

MARY: She's against it.

GEORGE: *(Over this)* To get through this.

JOYCE: Are you crazy?

HANNAH: *(Over this)* He'll take out loans. Kids take out loans.

JOYCE: Not that. Not that.

HANNAH: *(Over the end of this)* And some of that was even from your Mother. She 'gave' it to Paulie for his college.

GEORGE: She said she could afford it.

JOYCE: You're not doing that.

GEORGE: It's the only savings we have, Joyce.

*(Then)*

JOYCE: Mom, Dad's social security?

GEORGE: She gets half. She never really worked.

JOYCE: You *worked*.

GEORGE: Hannah checked, her home doesn't take Medicaid; there are other places.

HANNAH: You should see them, Joyce.

GEORGE: But even that…Hannah asked a friend who knows about this stuff—

HANNAH: She'd have to own nothing. So you plan for it. There are ways of planning for it. Too late now. We're trying to sell what we can.

GEORGE: Our first thought was to mortgage this house.

JOYCE: Your house, Mom? You'd agree to that?

PATRICIA: I would.

HANNAH: *(Over this)* But we can't, Joyce. It's already mortgaged.

JOYCE: What are you talking about?

PATRICIA: I don't know.

HANNAH: Patricia, you mortgaged it.

JOYCE: Dad paid off this house more than twenty years ago.

HANNAH: Your mother mortgaged it again.

GEORGE: *(Over this)* She just hadn't told us.

JOYCE: When?

PATRICIA: I don't know.

GEORGE: *(Over this)* We don't know yet. We don't know.

HANNAH: *(To* PATRICIA*)* It's a different kind. It has been paying you in installments. *(To* GEORGE*)* Isn't that how it works?

GEORGE: We thought that money, her checks, were from investments.

HANNAH: They've let her—maybe urged her, suckered her, to borrow even more. So there's interest now too to pay back on that. Whatever 'that' is... We don't know yet.

GEORGE: We don't really know how much of this house Mom owns anymore.

HANNAH: They make it so damn complicated.

GEORGE: I learned about this yesterday.

JOYCE: *(All sinking in)* Oh god, Mom... What were you thinking?

GEORGE: Joyce—

PATRICIA: I don't know, Joyce.

HANNAH: *(Over this)* George and your mother have a meeting with these mortgage people; the ones who do these kinds of mortgages. Next Wednesday in Poughkeepsie.

GEORGE: We'll learn then how much we'll need to buy it back. Pay back—of what she's been given. Borrowed. The interest on that.

HANNAH: Fees. The agent told George on the phone to: expect fees.

PATRICIA: *(To* HANNAH*)* What does he mean?

HANNAH: *(To* PATRICIA*)* We don't know.

JOYCE: We need talk to a lawyer.

GEORGE: Hannah and Mom have. She signed a contract.

PATRICIA: George went to high school with him, Joyce.

HANNAH: He did. So he didn't charge us anything.

JOYCE: How could this happen?

PATRICIA: *(Getting up)* George, I'm tired.

HANNAH: Let me help you.

JOYCE: She doesn't need help, Hannah.

GEORGE: You going to have a lie down? Watch some T V on the couch?

PATRICIA: Joyce is right. I don't need help… *(She heads to the living room.)*

GEORGE: It's good to have Joyce here, isn't it, Mom?

PATRICIA: It is. It always is.

*(As* PATRICIA *leaves:)*

HANNAH: George, if she's going to watch T V, she needs to remember to use both channel changers…

*(*GEORGE *starts to stand, stops:)*

GEORGE: Karin can help her.

MARY: This is hard on her.

*(As* PATRICIA *leaves:)*

GEORGE: Joyce, what if—Hannah and I rent out *our* house….?

JOYCE: What do you mean?

GEORGE: There's still a mortgage, but it's not that big. We could even take out another—

HANNAH: I told you I wouldn't be comfortable with that.

GEORGE: Start to pay off her debts with the rent money from our house. And any money from the things we're trying to sell. *(Beginning of a list)* Her car.

HANNAH: It's worth almost nothing.

GEORGE: We'll save by stopping the insurance. *(Next)* The piano… *(Then)* Some furniture…Mom has some jewelry…

MARY: Whatever Karin and I find that is worth anything…

GEORGE: So Mom moves back here to her house. Where she's comfortable.

HANNAH: She can do steps. She's still pretty healthy.

GEORGE: Hannah and I would then live here with Mom. And look after her.

JOYCE: *(Looks to* MARY*)* And Mary…?

MARY: I'll be moving to Pittsburg. Not right away, of course. When it starts to feel too crowded. And Karin's just month-to-month. She's knows all about this.

JOYCE: *(As it sinks in)* So she doesn't even own her house? How could this happen?

GEORGE: At least part of it. We don't know. She doesn't know. We'll know more on Wednesday.

JOYCE: Fuck.

GEORGE: Don't just say that. Don't just say, 'fuck.' We'll make it work. But we hear you. The last thing we touch—is Paulie's college… Okay?

JOYCE: Fuck! How could this happen? *(Then, to* GEORGE:*)* You know, I remember when Paulie was like ten hours old. And you're holding up a little booklet:

'Look, I'm opening up Paulie's college fund!' You were
so damn proud.

GEORGE: With like five dollars… Oh that was a real
smart investment… Put the money in the bank. Let
the interest just grow and grow… What the hell ever
happened to interest from a bank—?

JOYCE: You all know I don't have any money.

GEORGE: *(A joke)* Oh, now that's a surprise… *(Teasing)*
'You need to be more responsible, Joyce…' 'Grow up,
Joyce.'

JOYCE: *(Smiling)* Fuck you.

GEORGE: *(Smiling)* Everyone knows that, Joyce…
Everyone.

JOYCE: And the two girls I went around Europe with?
I didn't tell you this. I was embarrassed. And please,
don't tell Mom. They have goddamn trust funds. Who
knew? I'm in debt now to both of them… I thought we
were going to be traveling on the cheap…

*(PATRICIA enters on her way to the dining room.)*

HANNAH: *(Standing up)* You need something, Patricia?

JOYCE: We don't have to wait on her. She's not that old.

*(KARIN has entered right behind PATRICIA.)*

KARIN: Pat would like her sherry, she said.

JOYCE: *(To MARY)* Is there still sherry?

*(PATRICIA heads off.)*

MARY: Maybe a little. I haven't been buying it.

GEORGE: *(Looks at his watch)* I think it's that time,
Mom… It is that time.

MARY: You can come back in here, Karin. I think we're
finished. Are we finished?

GEORGE: Find anything we can sell? Any 'treasures'?

KARIN: Not yet... *(She goes.)*

GEORGE: *(To* JOYCE*)* We finished? For now?

JOYCE: Why didn't you tell me about the house?

HANNAH: He just learned this yesterday, Joyce.

GEORGE: We'll know more on Wednesday...

MARY: *(Changing the subject)* Joyce, have you been following Paulie on Facebook?

JOYCE: Of course.

MARY: So have we. Every day.

JOYCE: Does he know that?

GEORGE: *(Of course not)* No.

JOYCE: I can't believe my nephew's already in college...

HANNAH: You saw him graduate—.

JOYCE: I know...

MARY: Here's something that will make you laugh, Joyce. *(To* GEORGE*)* Tell your sister about you and Hannah taking Paulie to Purchase.

KARIN: *(Returning with the box, to* JOYCE*)* I've heard this. It's very funny.

HANNAH: You have? She has?

JOYCE: So you used to call Mom 'Pat?'

KARIN: No. No, I never did... *(She will look through the boxes.)*

MARY: *(To* GEORGE*)* Tell Joyce, she could use a laugh.

HANNAH: *(To* JOYCE*)* Did you know it was almost California...?

JOYCE: I know. You've told me ten times.

GEORGE: A state school—thank you god... Thank you!

JOYCE: What happened?

MARY: They bring Paulie to his dorm... *(To* HANNAH*)* Tell Joyce.

HANNAH: He didn't want us even to help. He wanted to say—goodbye Mom and Dad *(Looks to* GEORGE*)*—in the parking lot. Fortunately, we had a little refrigerator, so he needed 'Dad' to help carry it.

GEORGE: *(Laughs)* Three flights!

JOYCE: *(Laughs)* Oh god.

HANNAH: *(Continues)* We meet his roommate and his roommate's parents—*they're* sitting on the bed, they weren't rushed away by their son.

GEORGE: I think they were just oblivious. They seemed that sort of—

HANNAH: They were from some fancy place in Connecticut. They'd 'heard' of Rhinebeck. 'Friends' have weekend places in 'Rhinebeck'.

GEORGE: We were the *thoughtful* parents.

JOYCE: I'm sure you were.

*(*PATRICIA *returns with her sherry.)*

HANNAH: *(Over this)'*The new Hamptons' they called Rhinebeck, didn't they? I didn't just dream that?

JOYCE: I've heard that.

PATRICIA: I've heard that too. My god.

GEORGE: I wasn't as bothered as—

HANNAH: *(Over this)* I wasn't *bothered.* How people think of us. Rhinebeck...

JOYCE: I hear the same thing. Makes me cringe.

GEORGE: You going to sit there?

JOYCE: Mom, don't you want your chair??

MARY: Patricia, they're telling Joyce about taking Paulie to his college...

PATRICIA: Oh, this is a good story, Joyce…

HANNAH: You're going to spill that, Patricia.

GEORGE: *(Continuing)* We quickly said our goodbyes—
*we* were the good parents who took the hint. We leave
his dorm and before we head home, Hannah wants
to—

HANNAH: *(Over this)* Not just me.

GEORGE: —take a little stroll around the campus,
and— 'feel' what it's like? What it's going to be like for
*(Making fun, imitating* HANNAH*)* 'our little Paulie?'

JOYCE: *(To* PATRICIA*)* You all right?

HANNAH: *(Over this)* Come on, that's not fair. You too!

GEORGE: *(Over this)* We find a bench on a little path;
Hannah and I sit down and…what?
We just start—to cry. *(Laughter)* Tears gushing out.
Gushing. Both of us on this bench. 'How we miss our
boy.' I don't know all the crazy things we're saying
and saying them out loud, when—around the corner,
comes a whole gang of college kids, and who should be
right in the middle of the gang?

*(Laughter)*

JOYCE: No!

MARY: *(Explaining)* Paulie…

JOYCE: *(Over this)* It was his first day on his own. What
were you two thinking?

PATRICIA: You'd understand better if you had children,
Joyce.

GEORGE: Mom…

HANNAH: Patricia…

JOYCE: God, Mom…

MARY: Joyce, I think what you mother is trying to say is: she felt like that when you went to college. She told us this just the other day, that after you'd gone, she slept in your bed for about a week...

GEORGE: *(To* JOYCE*)* Did you know that?

*(Then)*

JOYCE: So—what did Paulie do?

HANNAH: Walked right past us, Joyce. And pretended he didn't know who the hell we were...

*(Lights fade.)*

## 4.
## George has a plan

*(The same, a short time later)*

*(*PATRICIA *sits, sips her sherry, watching all the activity around her:* MARY *continues to work on her casserole;* KARIN *continues to sort through the box of notebooks;* HANNAH *continues to prepare the potato salad; later she will prepare the dressing for a coleslaw.)*

*(All listen to* GEORGE *who is in the middle of telling a story, mostly to* JOYCE *[as the others have heard most of it].)*

GEORGE: Joyce, he writes to his publisher saying—he'll be done with his new book within a month. The book—is *Moby Dick.*

HANNAH: But he wasn't calling it that then—.

GEORGE: I think he was, Hannah. *Moby Dick.*

HANNAH: *(To* JOYCE*)* It was an entirely different book.

GEORGE: *(Over this)* Now Melville is taking a quick vacation up in the Berkshires. He's got relatives there, with a farm in Pittsfield. It's still there.

JOYCE: Is it?

HANNAH: *(Over this)* Part of a golf course. The clubhouse. *(Looks to* GEORGE*)*

GEORGE: When one day, while a few of his literary friends from New York are visiting—some writer, an editor—Melville and his pals get invited to a picnic. And it's the route of *this* picnic that we're going to be following tomorrow.

HANNAH: If it doesn't rain.

GEORGE: Even if it rains. It rained *then*.

HANNAH: I don't want to go if it's raining.

JOYCE: It's not going to rain.

GEORGE: *(Over this)* We're following the same route— of the most famous literary picnic in the history of American literature.

JOYCE: I don't know anything about this.

*(*MARY *stands to get some Paul Newman lemonade out of the refrigerator.)*

MARY: *(To* JOYCE*)* He's told us—. *(Her,* KARIN *and* PATRICIA*)*

JOYCE: *(To* HANNAH, *over this)* Why are you making a face?

GEORGE: The picnic where Herman Melville first met— Nathaniel Hawthorne.

JOYCE: Why don't I know this?

MARY: *(Holding up the Paul Newman)* Anyone?

*(No one wants any;* MARY *will pour herself a glass.)*

GEORGE: *After* this day, this picnic, Joyce, Herman Melville will throw away his nearly finished book, and start all over again. And for the next so many months, he will be consumed rewriting, rethinking, what we now know as—*Moby Dick. (Then)* Something happened that day. What happened?

HANNAH: What about Joyce's wine? Can we open that?

JOYCE: I stole it. Open it. Mom got to have her sherry.

HANNAH: George?

JOYCE: *(Confused)* And this guy knows what actually happened?

GEORGE: No. No. *(He gets up.)* Of course not.

JOYCE: *(To* HANNAH*)* I thought that's where this was headed. Stop making that face.

*(As* GEORGE *gets the wine out of the refrigerator; opens it:)*

GEORGE: Ignore her. Who knows what happened, Joyce. No one does. But something did happen. Tomorrow we're going to celebrate that.

JOYCE: *(To the women)* What's— '*that*'??? What are you celebrating??

GEORGE: *(Over this)* Before this picnic, Herman was just a self-taught writer of exotic sea tales. *After...?* Well he'll be different. Something will have set him free, and American literature will be changed forever. *(He goes to the sink for glasses.)*

JOYCE: *(To the women)* I've never read *Moby Dick*.

MARY: Me neither.

KARIN: I have.

JOYCE: Like all of the characters are men.

KARIN: *(Same time)* It's really long.

GEORGE: It takes place at sea, of course there are men. *(He has picked glasses out of the dishrack.)* These all right? *(Continues)* We have no description of the moment these two actually met. *(He holds glass up.)*

MARY: They should be clean.

GEORGE: They're fine.

*(*PATRICIA *is interested in one of the notebooks.)*

JOYCE: Find something, Mom?

PATRICIA: This one is all about Rhinebeck...

GEORGE: Mom, should I keep—? Joyce was asking me about the picnic. *(Continues)* Melville, very much wants to meet Hawthorne who is living now near Lennox—.

PATRICIA: Where Tanglewood—.

GEORGE: His house is still there. On the grounds.

HANNAH: It's been rebuilt two, three times.

PATRICIA: We used to go to Tanglewood... *(She stands up, picking up the notebooks.)*

HANNAH: *(To GEORGE)* Why don't we go anymore—?

GEORGE: Mom? What are you doing?

PATRICIA: I heard all about your picnic last night... *(She starts to head to the living room.)* May I borrow these, Mary?

MARY: Of course—.

JOYCE: *(Same time)* Where are you going?

HANNAH: *(To PATRICIA)* You okay?

JOYCE: To lie down, Hannah. She's tired.

PATRICIA: *(The notebooks)* They're all Thomas'?

MARY: They are. All his.

HANNAH: *(To GEORGE)* She going to lie on the couch?

*(GEORGE shrugs. PATRICIA is gone.)*

JOYCE: Restless... Like a ghost... 'Haunting us.'

HANNAH: Joyce...

JOYCE: I can say that, she's my mother.

HANNAH: No, you can't.

JOYCE: It's a joke.

MARY: Joyce, last night, at the restaurant—. Patricia said to me: how really sorry she was. How she'd fucked up.

JOYCE: Mom actually said 'fucked up?' Those words?

HANNAH: It's what she meant.

MARY: *(Working on her casserole)* How scared she was about seeing you today, Joyce.

JOYCE: Scared of me?

GEORGE: Didn't you know that?

*(Then)*

JOYCE: George, you were telling me about this picnic…

(MARY *sets the timer for preheating.)*

JOYCE: So what happened?

HANNAH: They don't know.

JOYCE: I know nothing about this.

GEORGE: *(Over this)* Hawthorne and his family are living full time near Lennox where he's trying to avoid a woman in town named Sedgwick. Also a writer. Best seller after best seller. His sales pale in comparison. He can't stand her.

HANNAH: He (GEORGE) likes the *gossip*.

GEORGE: It's not gossip. It's history. Sedgwick's brother, Hawthorne's Boston publisher, Fields, and *the* Doctor Oliver Holmes. They're the other picnickers.

HANNAH: And two women. That's why I have to go.

GEORGE: The wife of the publisher.

HANNAH: *(To* JOYCE, *as she shreds the carrots)* That's me. She wore a blue silk dress. I don't own a blue silk dress.

JOYCE: What are you going to wear?

HANNAH: It's cotton. It's blue…

JOYCE: I think this sounds like fun.

HANNAH: *(Smiles)* Fuck you.

JOYCE: *(To* HANNAH*)* Any kind of hat?

HANNAH: I don't wear hats.

GEORGE: They drive together in one carriage the few miles south to the base of Monument Mountain.

HANNAH: *(Teasing George, to* JOYCE*)* It's still there.

GEORGE: Unload hampers of food and champagne.

HANNAH: They're bringing antique straw hampers. I'm bringing Tupperware.

GEORGE: *(Over this, continuing)* And then begin the climb. It's not that difficult a walk—. *(Looks to* HANNAH*)* The women are fine. They follow a ridge. Nathaniel, we know, was a very reserved man. He walks a little ahead of the group, as the others, in party-mood, make up rhymes, puns fly in every direction-

HANNAH: *(To* JOYCE*)* Sounds like so much fun, doesn't it?

GEORGE: And that gets the party going. 'So tell me about life in Concord,' Herman asks his idol. 'Well,' Hawthorne says, 'with Thoreau, you just feel embarrassed talking money… Emerson on the other hand, he sued to get his share of his first wife's inheritance;

*(Timer goes off.)*

GEORGE: —he's got bank and railroad stock now. Longfellow—he's making a hundred bucks a week from *Evangeline.*

JOYCE: So they just talked money?

HANNAH: According to George's new best friend. The guy worked on Wall Street.

(MARY *will put the casserole into the oven to bake; set the timer again:*)

GEORGE: Somehow Melville's arm got around the older man's shoulders. This surprises everyone; Nathaniel Hawthorne did not like to be touched. The picnickers reach the summit and our two men sit apart and talk.

HANNAH: *(To* JOYCE*)* We don't know what about.

GEORGE: We know from letters that Hawthorne tells Melville that he has stopped reading newspapers.

JOYCE: Was it an election year?

GEORGE: They talk about life insurance, how neither can afford such a thing. And how America 'tames' its artists. When Melville suddenly stands and runs out onto a jutting rock and pretends to be on the bowsprit of a ship, hauling in imaginary ropes. All the time shouting orders to the wind, making his new friend laugh.

HANNAH: *(Explains)* He's drunk.

GEORGE: No one can believe it, when Nathaniel follows his friend onto the jutting rock and shouts to the whole world — that he has found the 'great carbuncle.'

JOYCE: *(To* HANNAH*)* What is that?

HANNAH: Who knows?

GEORGE: *(Over this)* A thunderstorm sweeps across the mountain top; the group finds sanctuary under some protruding cliff; our two friends stand together, soaked, lightning flashes, rolls of thunder, rain whips, as the two men shout into the dark sky...

*(Then)*

JOYCE: What did they shout?

HANNAH: We don't know... So that's what we're
doing tomorrow. George and me and George's new
rich friend, and the rich friend's rich friends... *(To
Joyce)* Taste it, tell me what you think. *(Of the coleslaw)*
Doesn't it sound like a good time?

GEORGE: It could be fun.

HANNAH: I think it needs more mustard.

JOYCE: So you really don't know what happened?

HANNAH: No. No one does.

GEORGE: We know that from that day on American
literature—

HANNAH: I think she's heard enough.

JOYCE: How did you meet this guy?

HANNAH: George met him in the Millerton diner.

GEORGE: He and his wife were in the next booth.

HANNAH: *(This explains everything)* They have a
weekend place up here.

KARIN: That Diner? It's near Hotchkiss...I go there for
lunch sometimes.

HANNAH: *(Over this)* That diner's— *(Makes quotation
marks with her fingers)* 'authentic' country. *(As if this
explains everything)* If you're from the city.

*(MARY will head off to the mud room, to collect vegetables
for a vegetable marinade.)*

KARIN: *(To MARY)* It gets crowded.

GEORGE: *(Continues)* And we got to talking, Joyce; I said
I'd spent my whole life here. And he said how rare that
was these days to find someone like me. *(Smiles, then)*
That was nice to hear. We got started talking about
the area, its history, and he said he really wanted one
day to walk in the steps of the most famous literary
picnic—which of course 'as you know' happened only

a few miles away. I didn't know. *(To* JOYCE*)* Did you know?

*(*MARY *returns with mushrooms, cauliflower, tomatoes, green beans, and an avocado.)*

JOYCE: So then your new friend invited you on his picnic.

HANNAH: He's 'retired'. He's like forty years old.

GEORGE: He's done all this research.

HANNAH: He has an assistant who seems to do most of it.

GEORGE: *(Lists)* What they ate. The poems they read that day...

HANNAH: They'll eat whatever tomorrow.

KARIN: *(To* MARY*)* Let me do *something.* I've just been sitting here...

HANNAH: You're finding treasure... That's important.

MARY: Karin, if you want, you can help me cut up vegetables...

*(*KARIN *starts to stand.)*

MARY: Let me just wash some of this first...

HANNAH: *(To* JOYCE*)* Your mother has a hummus mix...God knows how old it is. What the hell... *(She heads to the cupboard.)* I don't care how old it is... As long as it's easy. *(Incredible, about* GEORGE*)* He promised them hummus.

JOYCE: Did they eat hummus? Hawthorne and Melville?

HANNAH: Did they, George?

GEORGE: *(Ignoring them)* We're going to read the poems tomorrow. He has the original books. He has a book dealer who finds him these things.

(HANNAH *gets the box of hummus mix.*)

(MARY *is washing the vegetables.*)

HANNAH: *(To* JOYCE*)* Here… There are directions. You can make it right in the Tupperware. I'll get the…

(HANNAH *will get a tupperware container for* JOYCE.*)*

GEORGE: Last night he also told me something he just learned. Listen to this: when Herman goes to visit Nathaniel a few weeks later at Tanglewood?

MARY: *(A joke)* It must have been out of season, because the traffic gets—.

GEORGE: Herman regales *(Him)* —.

MARY: 'Regales.'

*(As* JOYCE *reads the directions on the box of hummus mix:)*

GEORGE: —regales him *and* Mrs Hawthorne with stories of south sea adventures—Mrs Hawthorne wrote a letter about this—and describes the *sex* customs of the natives.

*(They pay attention to this)*

GEORGE: Maybe his own experiences of sex with the natives…? *Then* exactly nine months later, Mrs. Hawthorne gives birth. *(The point)* Nine months later.

KARIN: *(To* MARY*)* Tell me how you want…?

MARY: It's a marinade. Just cut them up…

(KARIN *works with* MARY *on the vegetables for the marinade.*)

JOYCE: *(Over this)* Are you saying that Melville was the father of Hawthorne's— *(Children)*?

GEORGE: That's not what I'm saying, Joyce.

(MARY *wipes the mushrooms clean.*)

MARY: That's what I thought he was saying too.

GEORGE: *(Over the end of this)* It was the 'excitement' of his stories that night...

KARIN: Now *that* would be interesting, if—

JOYCE: *(Agreeing)* If he had sex with Hawthorne's—.

GEORGE: Melville didn't have sex with Hawthorne's wife! Forget it.

KARIN: How do we know?

GEORGE: We just do. Come on. *(To HANNAH)* And please don't say things like that tomorrow.

*(They work. JOYCE on the hummus mix; she will need to get a measuring cup, water from the sink and oil. MARY and KARIN work on the vegetable marinade.)*

HANNAH: Tell your sister about his weekend house.

JOYCE: What about...?

GEORGE: I know, Hannah, but—.

HANNAH: George's new rich friend bought this old house in Stockbridge. Very 'historic'. And he's been fixing it up. He has people fixing it up. We're hoping that George can be one of those people fixing it up.

JOYCE: So—you're 'networking'. Good for you.

GEORGE: That's not the only reason—.

JOYCE: I didn't think you had that in you.

*(GEORGE is pouring himself another glass of wine.)*

HANNAH: It's why we're going. *(About the wine)* George... *(Continues)* He buys his 'historic' house— last winter? He's hardly lived in it. He has some other houses too. The first thing he does is hire scene painters, theater people, to paint each room in a sort of 'scene.' *(begins to list the scenes)* A forest... *(To KARIN)* You knew one of them.

KARIN: I did.

HANNAH: So you sit in the living room and you're in a forest…

GEORGE: You haven't been—.

HANNAH: You told me. *(Continues the list)* Another room: a castle. What else?

*(No response)*

HANNAH: It's funny. They worked for months. And he and his wife arrive in July, from their house in Italy? And they love it. Love everything about it. They sit there in the forest; they have drinks in the 'castle'. He puts on monks chanting music. He 'loves' the 'feel' of history.

GEORGE: Hannah—.

HANNAH: *(Over this)* And two days later, the wife says— 'these rooms make me dizzy, like I want to throw up…'

JOYCE: Were the painters still— *(There)*?

KARIN: My friend was still there. Living above someone's garage. That's where he got put.

HANNAH: *(Over this)* So they then paint over everything. The same painters. Over all their work. This time— 'light blue'. 'Egg shell white…' So now they want—bookcases. Floor to ceiling. And built-in cabinets. All looking 'old.' *(In the guy's voice)* 'Really old.' 'That literary-cabin look.' Right? What the hell does that mean? But it'll be a big job. Probably take all winter for a good high-end carpenter… *(To* JOYCE*)* That's why we're going on this picnic… *(Looks to* GEORGE*)* Tell her… That's George's plan. Like *that*, he thinks he'll get enough work for the year.

GEORGE: And pay for Mom… What she owes. Maybe she could even stay in the Inn a couple more months… Start to pay off the mortgage…

JOYCE: You're a good carpenter.

GEORGE: A job like this can—.

HANNAH: He doesn't know for sure what it's going to pay. Rich people often don't pay well.

GEORGE: They don't just come along every day. Jobs like this.

HANNAH: *(Continuing)* We know that from experience.

GEORGE: It'd be steady work and for at least the entire winter. Probably longer. Everything custom.

HANNAH: If it works out.

MARY: Tell her what you're really worried about, Hannah.

JOYCE: What?

MARY: That his new friend really only wants George along—because George is a big guy—so he can carry a lot of the stuff for them up the mountain. At this picnic.

GEORGE: *(To HANNAH)* I told you I don't think that's true. I don't think that's fair.

HANNAH: *(Over this)* He sees a strong guy. A 'local'.

GEORGE: Hannah—

HANNAH: You know, so like on a safari…

JOYCE: A porter?? George, as their porter??

HANNAH: *(Demonstrating)* Carrying their baskets on his head? All the other picnickers are coming from New York City. Manhattan. Does he know you have a pacemaker, George?

JOYCE: *(To GEORGE)* Does he? Does he, George?

HANNAH: No.

GEORGE: We're just their guests.

HANNAH: Are we?

MARY: And after George mentions to his new rich friend that his wife does catering, Hannah too suddenly gets invited on this picnic...

HANNAH: And I get an email with a list of all the stuff they want me to cook...

*(Then)*

JOYCE: *(To* HANNAH*)* Are they paying you to...?

HANNAH: No. No. Of course not, Joyce.

*(Lights fade.)*


## 5.
## Joyce's trip abroad

*(The same; a short time later)*

*(*MARY *and* KARIN *prepare the vegetable marinade,* JOYCE *has paused from making the hummus mix;* HANNAH *continues to clean up;* GEORGE *is finishing his wine.)*

*(*JOYCE, *in the middle of conversation with* KARIN*:)*

JOYCE: Karin, I'd never worked with opera singers before...

GEORGE: *(Standing, about the dinner)* What can I do? What do you want me to do? I can help...

MARY: George, I think we have everything under— *(Control)*

HANNAH: Let him do something. He wants to.

GEORGE: I'm not helpless in the kitchen.

JOYCE: Help your wife. With your 'picnic'.

GEORGE: I don't want to get in her way.

JOYCE: *(Joking)* That's always a good excuse...

HANNAH: Ignore your sister. *(Handing him a large index card with a recipe)* Here... Help with this. O K?

KARIN: *(To* MARY*)* 'O K.' 'Old Kinderhook…'
'Rhinebeck'.

GEORGE: *(Taking the card)* Her guacamole.

JOYCE: Guacamole. You're really going to trust him
with that?

MARY: *(Defending him)* He cooks.

JOYCE: *(About the recipe)* Follow this, George. Ask if you
have questions. It's not a crime to ask questions…

MARY: *(Again)* He cooks, Joyce.

*(*GEORGE *reads the recipe.)*

KARIN: *(To* JOYCE*)* What were you saying? About opera
singers…

*(*GEORGE *looks over the table, seeing what ingredients for his
guacamole are already out.)*

HANNAH: He's fine, Joyce.

KARIN: About your opera in London…

JOYCE: *(Continuing)* The singers' corsets, Karin…I really
thought we were going to get big resistance to them.

KARIN: Because of the… *(Chest)*

JOYCE: *(Over this)* But they took to the corsets like… No
problem.

KARIN: Did they think it helped their singing?

MARY: *(Giving* KARIN *the word)* The diaphragm?

JOYCE: *(To* KARIN*)* I thought maybe that. But the
costume shop head, she's been at the E N O like
forever…I happened to say how I'd been worried
about the corsets. After all, they must be terribly
uncomfortable. 'So?' she said. 'How comfortable are
your high heels, Joyce? And the hours spent putting
on your makeup? It's sexy. It's fun. Makes you feel—
different. Like you're ready for something…'

KARIN: It can feel like that. She's right. *(To the others)* Can't it?

*(GEORGE stands.)*

GEORGE: Mary, you keep the vegetables... *(Out in the mudroom)*

MARY: In the mudroom.

*(GEORGE heads for the mudroom.)*

JOYCE: You want help? Ask...

*(GEORGE is gone.)*

MARY: *(To HANNAH)* He'll find what he needs.

KARIN: *(To JOYCE)* It does sometimes makes me feel like that. Mary?

MARY: What? Sure.

JOYCE: She said: 'I'll tell you something that will surprise you. Did you know that *tight-lacing* of corsets—' *(Explains)* That's where you really pull—.

KARIN: I guessed that. I know that.

HANNAH: *(To MARY)* You want to show him what you want him to use?

MARY: He's fine...

*(HANNAH will join the women, and work on the vegetable marinade.)*

JOYCE: *(Continues)* 'Women who did that, they were seen by men as 'fast' girls...' *(Explains)* As women 'asserting' themselves. Wanting to be 'educated'. 'Meddlers' they were called.

HANNAH: Really? 'Who do they think they are?'

JOYCE: They were women wanting to 'show off.' Their power.

KARIN: Heels do that. I know that. *(To MARY and HANNAH)* Am I the only one...?

MARY: No, no.

HANNAH: *(Same time)* No.

JOYCE: So a lot of the people—the men—who were
against corsets, they tried to say their 'movement' was
about 'freeing' women from these 'terrible bonds.'
That was bullshit, she said. They were just a bunch of
conservative men afraid of women.

*(GEORGE returns with a few avocados, a couple of tomatoes,
etc. he will find a knife, a bowl, etc.)*

JOYCE: They encouraged women to wear nice
loose dresses that wouldn't call attention to what's
underneath...

KARIN: The simple loose dress.

MARY: Hear that, Hannah?

JOYCE: What?

HANNAH: Shut up.

MARY: She's always looking for that simple loose dress;
that she can wear to a fancy party, and can also garden
in. I keep telling her: *(To* HANNAH*)* there-is-no-such-
dress.

*(HANNAH holds out a knife to GEORGE.)*

GEORGE: I like this one... *(The one he has)*

JOYCE: *(Continues)* These men spread rumors about
women in their corsets—how in order to wear them
so tight they'd had their ribs removed. There are
newspaper articles that say that. See—these men tried
to turn them into freaks. *(To* HANNAH, *what to have with
the hummus)* With crudités?

HANNAH: I've got chips.

KARIN: This is interesting... *(To* MARY *and* HANNAH*)*
You've heard all this?

HANNAH: She's told us about her trip, moment by moment by moment... *(Looks to* MARY*)*

JOYCE: Karin asked. If I'm boring you—.

KARIN: *(Over this)* I'm interested. I'm an actress.

HANNAH: *(Over this)* One woman, Karin... *(To* JOYCE*)* You told us this... She got into the Guinness book of records—

JOYCE: She had a thirteen-inch waist. That's like this. *(Demonstrates)* This was in the Fifties.

KARIN: That's anorexia. That's not power.

JOYCE: *(Still demonstrating)* Like this!

MARY: I had patients with anorexia. My daughter went through that.

*(*GEORGE *will get ingredients in the refigerator, the cabinet.)*

HANNAH: You never talk about your daughter. I didn't know that.

MARY: Thank god she got over that... It was awful. My ex had no idea how to deal with her. One of the few times he actually called me for advice. Someone very wise had told me years before, the anorexic, she—

KARIN: Is it only girls?

MARY: It can be boys. But way more girls. The anorexic she is just trying to move some psychological '*stress*'— into a physical stress, because *that* she thinks she can bear. Because it's physical.

*(They work, then)*

JOYCE: *(Continues)* This woman in the costume shop, she gave me this complicated 'explanation' about how clothes and sexual desire are inseparable.

HANNAH: I think she was trying to pick you up.

KARIN: *(Smiling)* Oh I agree, Joyce.

JOYCE: Maybe.

HANNAH: *(To* MARY*)* She was trying to pick her up.

JOYCE: *(Over this)* That sexual desire with a man, she said, there's obviously a pursuit toward a single-minded goal, a happy 'release'…

GEORGE: *(Without looking up)* Sounds about right.

JOYCE: And collapse, and then…from zero again.

KARIN: Boy is that true.

JOYCE: But with a woman—I can see her telling me this smoking her third cigarette in a row—.

MARY: You can smoke in—?

JOYCE: We were in an alley alongside the E N O. But with a woman, it's all entwined with what she is 'thinking'. It's blended together, so *potentially* there's this desire that is always 'on tap.'

HANNAH: *(To* MARY*)* 'On tap.'

JOYCE: And that desire is what we clothe.

HANNAH: *(To* GEORGE, *peeling avocadoes)* You're doing great.

GEORGE: I know.

JOYCE: *(To the others, an endearment, about* GEORGE*)* 'Our cookerer…' Helping out 'the women…'

HANNAH: Ignore your sister.

GEORGE: *(As if he didn't hear)* What?

JOYCE: *(Continuing)* She said women instinctively know this.

KARIN: That the desire is always on tap.

JOYCE: We see the world through this lens. And that's why women make such damn good costume designers.

HANNAH: She was flattering you. Did she know you were only the associate designer?

JOYCE: She knew.

KARIN: *(Over this)* I see what she's saying. The best costume designers are women, I think. That's been my experience.

JOYCE: Every piece of clothing can *mean* something. As designers, we try to control or determine this meaning. What's trying to be said. Or better, what we're trying to hide.

KARIN: What the character is trying to hide? Is that what you mean?

JOYCE: I think so.

MARY: I don't think I understand.

JOYCE: Mary, let's say you're cast in a play.

HANNAH: Oh I'd like to see that.

MARY: Be quiet.

JOYCE: *(Over this)* And I'm costuming you. So I study the character you're to play. First, what does she want to hide? That's always a good place to begin. And, then I look to you, Mary the person; and ask the same thing. What are you hiding?

MARY: You mean what I don't like about myself?

KARIN: That's part of it, of course.

HANNAH: You're a fucking costume associate, not a psychiatrist.

JOYCE: *(To KARIN)* Is there much difference?

KARIN: Sometimes there really isn't.

JOYCE: Follow me around for a day, Hannah. Go with my boss to a fitting. When she gets going: it's transfixing.

KARIN: The really good ones are like that, Hannah.

JOYCE: *(Over this, lists)* The actor is trying to get her to notice what the actor wants her to notice. *And* also not notice. What the actor wants to hide, about herself. What's underneath. My boss said the other day, it's like pulling up a mat or rug that's been outside, and suddenly there's all this life underneath. So much that we never see. Instead, we seem to live our lives painting everything in these broad, obvious brushstrokes. Everyone is either this, or that. The 'lawyer', she wears a suit. The 'jock', she is in shorts. But people are much more than that, she said. And so of course—much more interesting... *(Shrugs)* She can drive me crazy at times—.

KARIN: I should show Joyce what I was reading to you this morning... People are more than what they want us to see.

HANNAH: What?

KARIN: Edith...

HANNAH: Oh you should get that—

MARY: Get it. Get it.

GEORGE: What?

(KARIN, *standing up, wiping her hands on her apron, to* JOYCE:)

KARIN: You're sure?

JOYCE: What are you talking about?

HANNAH: This is really hidden.

KARIN: I've been working on a one-woman show, Joyce...

MARY: *(Over this)* Just get it.

KARIN: I left it in the living room...

MARY: I saw it next to the T V...

*(As* KARIN *heads off)*

MARY: And check on Patricia.

JOYCE: *(Over this)* Edith?

MARY: You'll see... It's a surprise.

HANNAH: *(To* JOYCE*)* I agree, people are more than what they want us to see.

JOYCE: I saw a show about fans in Paris. How there were codes and hidden meanings. An entire language of fans. The Eighteenth century.

MARY: A language...?

JOYCE: There were fans that on one side had, say, an idyllic rural scene, fauna; and on the other—a naked couple copulating. Completely pornographic.

HANNAH: And...?

JOYCE: So the woman fanning herself, if she were interested, would simply flip the fan, for an instant, showing the man the other side... And then he'd know...

*(*KARIN, *with the book.)*

KARIN: George, your mother can't get the television to work...

*(*GEORGE *starts to get up.)*

GEORGE: I'm coming, Mom. I'll help you...

HANNAH: You need to use both channel changers. First the big one then the little. It took me forever to learn that.

GEORGE: *(Goes to the sink to wash his hands)* The order doesn't matter, Hannah.

*(They see* PATRICIA *entering from living room.)*

HANNAH: I thought it did.

PATRICIA: I don't want to watch T V. *(With the notebooks)* Here…Mary his handwriting gets hard to read.

MARY: That happened, Patricia. I know. I know. I got used to it. I can read some things to you.

PATRICIA: What can I do?

MARY: The casserole's already in the oven, Patricia. I think we have everything under control. Hannah, do you need more help with the picnic?

HANNAH: I think I'm fine, Patricia.

MARY: You found the book?

KARIN: *(Holding up the book, about* PATRICIA*)* Is this all right for Pat to…?

GEORGE: Sit down with me, Mom. You can watch me make guacamole…

PATRICIA: It that an interesting thing to watch?

HANNAH: Join us, Patricia. Let me clear some space… Joyce has been telling us more about her trip to Europe.

PATRICIA: I'd like to hear more about that, Joyce… *(She has sat at the table.)*

JOYCE: What's to tell? And Karin was just about to read us something…

KARIN: We don't have to do that.

JOYCE: What are you going to read?

KARIN: Mary?

GEORGE: You okay, Mom?

KARIN: *(To* MARY*)* You sure this all right?

JOYCE: What? Something from some 'Edith.' Who's Edith?

KARIN: *(Showing the cover)* Edith — Wharton…

62                     WHAT DID YOU EXPECT?

JOYCE: Mom, you've read her.

PATRICIA: I have.

GEORGE: *(Working)* She lived in Rhinebeck for a while. *(To* PATRICIA, *as a joke)* Did you know her, Mom?

*(*PATRICIA *likes the joke.)*

MARY: Hannah?

HANNAH: Karin's going to do this play, Patricia—. She's an actress.

PATRICIA: I know.

HANNAH: *(Over this)* It's a little risqué.

JOYCE: I'm interested.

KARIN: Mary?

*(*MARY *shrugs)*

KARIN: Well, you see photos of Wharton—fur collar, prim, big hat. The picture of a proper lady. With all emotions—pretty much kept at their proper distance. So that's the woman I was planning on portraying. But then, I was telling Mary and Hannah that I came across this—.

MARY: Something she wrote.

HANNAH: We found it funny.

KARIN: —in the back of a biography. Never before published. Probably, they think, left unfinished… *(Opens the book)* I'll just read a little of it… *(Hesitates, looks at* MARY *and* HANNAH*)*

GEORGE: *(Confused, to* HANNAH*)* What?

KARIN: Where should I start…? *(Reads)* "The room was warm and softly lit…. 'Now my darling,' Mr Palmato said. She let herself sink backward among the pillows…her lips were parted by his tongue. Her nipples as hard as coral, but sensitive as lips to his approaching touch... His hand softly separated her legs, and began to slip up the old path it had so often traveled in darkness." *(She looks up, then continues to read.)* "But now it was light, she was uncovered, and looking downward, she could see her own parted knees and outstretched ankles and feet... And his hand... *(Corrects herself)* As his hand stole higher she felt the bud swelling and burst into bloom. His fore-finger pressing it, forcing its petals apart, and laying on their sensitive edges a circular touch...."

HANNAH: *(To* PATRICIA*)* Are you okay with this?

PATRICIA: Are you?

KARIN: "... letting herself downward along the divan," I jumped a little, *(Continues)* "until her head was in line with his middle, she began to caress it, with her tongue. She wound her caresses deeper and deeper into the thick firm folds, until, in a thrice—." That's the only thing that makes it seem old: 'thrice,' "– in a thrice it was withdrawn, her knees pressed apart, and she felt it descend on her and plunge into the depths of her thirsting body..." That's probably a good place to stop. *(Closes the book)*

JOYCE: Hannah...?

HANNAH: *(To* JOYCE*)* It was funnier this morning...

JOYCE: Mom, you okay?

*(*PATRICIA *finds reading glasses, reaches for the book from* KARIN.*)*

What? *(As a joke)* You think you missed something, Mom? *(Smiles)* Why are you so interested? I'm really surprised.

PATRICIA: Joyce, why wouldn't I be? *(Opens the book)*

KARIN: There's a photo of her, the year she wrote that. It's in the middle of the book. She was nearly fifty. She

looks completely different than in any of her other
photos. All the stiff stuff around her neck is gone.
She shows some cleavage… What she'd been hiding
inside…

JOYCE: Oh Edith.

MARY: When I'd just left med school, and doing
my first residency. I still thought I'd end up doing
research.

JOYCE: What are you—?

MARY: This relates to that.

HANNAH: You never talk about yourself. She never
talks about herself.

PATRICIA: *(Looks up from the book)* I know.

MARY: That's not true. I talk about myself all the time.
*(Then) To* myself. *(Cont'd)* I was good at research. I
liked the order of things. You start with x, you do the
experiment over and over. It's hard to get lost. I think I
was scared of that. Feeling lost.

JOYCE: I understand that.

KARIN: Me too.

HANNAH: Who doesn't understand that?

MARY: There was a senior doctor. A wise man. He
said—and no one ever told me this in med school—
he said: above all else, Mary, besides paying close
attention to your patient. Listen to what is beyond
or *behind* what he says. Try and enter into his or her
stories, his or her predicaments; and *then* try and be
*them.* Get *inside* them. *(Looks up)* We were talking about
how you can never know what's inside people… *(Then)*
When I first met Thomas—this is now years later—one
day I tell him about what this doctor had told me. And
how what he had said changed my life and made me
understand the *complexity* of being a doctor. *And* the

joy. The whole art of observing… And I told Thomas about a paper I had even helped write—how doctors can learn so much about their patients, from just watching: the way they walk, stand, sit… Thomas said to me, 'Mary, just like theater.'

OTHERS: 'Of course.' 'Theater!' 'What else?'

*(Then)*

JOYCE: What about *your* license, Mary?

HANNAH: I don't think she has done anything yet.

JOYCE: You're renewing your doctor's license.

HANNAH: After five years, she thinks they'll make her take all the tests again.

JOYCE: You doing that?

HANNAH: Will you do that?

JOYCE: Are you?

MARY: Maybe, Hannah. Maybe. But I should never have let it expire. That was stupid of me.

HANNAH: You were taking care of Thomas.

MARY: I know… But now? *(Then)* Talking about watching people, and listening to them… Thomas and I once had the great good fortune to meet a very special man, a doctor. I don't think I ever told you this, Hannah.

HANNAH: I didn't know.

MARY: Neurologist. He died last year. God bless him. He'd seen two of Thomas' plays, and he too loved the theater; so he agreed to see us. I thought maybe Thomas' condition about being able to walk to music was fairly unique—it's not. There are plenty of other examples with Parkinson's. But we went to his office in the West Village on Horatio; and spent an hour or so together. *(Incredible:)* How *that man watched*. That was art. *(Then)* When he died, someone wrote about him—that as with all the very greatest doctors, his most essential clinical instrument—was his heart. *(Smiles)* That day with Thomas, this great man took me aside and told me: when you look at those who suffer, he said, who have taken life's hardest hits... Try not to see them as in any way diminished, but rather as our warriors, Mary, our tragic heroes, struggling across the abyss...

*(Lights fade.)*

## 6.
## Thomas

*(The same; a short time later)*

*(MARY, JOYCE, and HANNAH work on the vegetable marinade and hummus.)*

*(GEORGE works on his guacamole. PATRICIA listens.)*

*(KARIN having gone back into the box of notebooks and books, she now holds a book:)*

KARIN: *This* book has your name, George, in it...

JOYCE: That means nothing in this house. As a kid George wrote his name in everything... A really nasty habit, wasn't it, Mom?

GEORGE: I was like six years old, Joyce.

JOYCE: *(Working)* Thomas got so fed up with that—

MARY: I don't think I know this.

HANNAH: I do.

JOYCE: —so Thomas convinced George to write his name in one of Dad's *Penthouse* magazines.

GEORGE: It wasn't funny. It really wasn't.

JOYCE: Not to you.

HANNAH: And that's why Patricia, you started calling…

PATRICIA: What?

JOYCE: You still do.

HANNAH: *(Over this)*"Put your '*George*' right there…" *(To* PATRICIA*)* You always say it when you want someone to sign something.

PATRICIA: I do?

MARY: *(Over this)* That's why. I never knew that.

HANNAH: You did it just yesterday, with Mary's birthday card. 'Put your George…'

KARIN: That's what that was.

MARY: In my family — there was an uncle who always said things without thinking.

HANNAH: You had just one of those?

MARY: *(Over this)* I'm maybe twelve, and he's visiting my parents, and he comes out of the bathroom and holds up to me—for some reason to me—an empty toilet roll and says, 'Mary? Mary?' And I guess I'm supposed to get for him a new roll of toilet paper. But what everyone else only sees is my Uncle holding up this empty, and shouting 'Mary!' For some reason that was funny. And from that day on an empty toilet roll, in my family, will forever be called 'a Mary.' Thomas loved that story. He even used it in one of his plays. He didn't call her 'Mary.'

KARIN: *(With a airmail one-sheet letter in hand)* Maybe here's something… This is interesting. An airmail letter. It's from a painter. Kitaj…?

JOYCE: Who?

KARIN: Isn't he famous?

GEORGE: Kitaj. I know who that is.

MARY: *(Over)* To Thomas?

KARIN: No, no. Wait. 'Sandra' —she's obviously
the wife. And this painter blames her death on his
critics, on other artists… *(Reads)* "I will always believe
that her stroke and death (in one weekend thank
God)…" *(Skims)* "the personal hatreds towards me…"
"savages…" "I still break down after six months. And
to think she never saw the Met show—"

GEORGE: *(To* HANNAH*)* He had a show at the Met.

KARIN: "—and the Kitaj flag flying there…" Do you say
it 'Kit-I' or Kit-agg?' I've heard both.

GEORGE: I don't know. I know his paintings…

JOYCE: I know them too…

KARIN: *(Reads)* "The Met! Who could have thought
such a thing when we were kids at Cooper?" He's
writing to old friends. *(Looks at postmark)* Sent from
London. 'May 1995.'

HANNAH: *(To* KARIN*) Where* was this?

KARIN: It was just inside this notebook. In this baggie…

MARY: *(Taking the baggie)* He kept his valuable things in
these…

GEORGE: So Thomas knew it was valuable.

KARIN: *(Reads)* "We sure have our share of tsouris…"
that's a Yiddish word. *(Skims)* "The whole thing is
monstrous…" "My life has been hellish… Sandra lit up
everyone's life with her beauty, both inside and out."
"My 10 year old Max…" So they had a son.

JOYCE: *(To* GEORGE*)* 'Ten years', Sandra couldn't have
been that old.

KARIN: *(Reads)* "When the clouds part, let's have a good
cry together, meanwhile, I'd like to be with Sandra…
wherever she is, but Max needs me, so I've become her

as well as me. Love and hugs and kisses, dear, dear friends, ever Kitaj…' Or Kitaj. *(Kitag)*

MARY: *(With a newspaper clipping from the bag)* A clipping about him… Looks like from *The Times*…

JOYCE: That's *The Times*. Is he still alive? Do we know?

GEORGE: I think he died just a couple of years ago. A very good painter. Maybe a great one… May I see?

*(KARIN hands him the letter.)*

MARY: Thomas' handwriting… *(Reads, from a note found in the baggie)* "Kitaj letter to good friends. Found inside the Tate catalogue of Kitaj's/Kitaj's *(Kitag)* show; in a used bookshop slash coffee shop in New Haven."

HANNAH: What do you think it's worth? Karin?

KARIN: *(Shrugs)* I know theater…

HANNAH: *(To GEORGE)* It must be worth something. Handwritten. He's very well known… Like a peek into his broken heart… People collect that…

MARY: Wait. *(Reads)* "Try to return to the son."

HANNAH: What??

MARY: Thomas wrote that: *(Shows them)* "Try to return to the son… Too private and too personal to sell." In caps: 'PLEASE DO NOT SELL.' *(Shows them)*

*(No one knows what to say.)*

PATRICIA: We're not going to sell that?

GEORGE: I don't think so, Mom…

*(Phone is ringing off.)*

HANNAH: Phone…

PATRICIA: *(Standing)* I'll get it…

GEORGE: Mom.

HANNAH: George…

PATRICIA: I will get it; it's my house... (*She moves slowly.*)

GEORGE: (*Wiping his hands*) Let me come with you, Mom...

PATRICIA: I don't need help.

HANNAH: George...

GEORGE: Let me just get past you, Mom, and get the phone...

(GEORGE *hurries past* PATRICIA *to get the phone; she follows.*)

MARY: I'll research and see if I can find the son. (*She takes the letter and folds it and puts it back in the baggie.*)

KARIN: I told Thomas he should put this in a play. One year I was watching the Tony Awards with Thomas.

MARY: Where—?

KARIN: In Brooklyn. This is sort of the same thing. Like 'Mary' the toilet roll. We had a mouse problem. So Thomas set a few traps under the sink. We're watching the Tonys, and—what's the name of that show?—where he's singing, '*I am what I am*'? Anyway, right at the climax of the song; the guy's singing full out: '*I am what I am!*'

(*Piano music off; Bach aria, played haltingly.*)

KARIN: We hear, under the sink: snap. Then—flap. Flap... Then...flap... Whenever I hear that song—that's what I hear—flap.

(GEORGE *returns:*)

GEORGE: It's the opera singer from Bard. She wants to come—

MARY: (*Suddenly*) Who's playing the piano?!

GEORGE: What??

HANNAH: *(Concerned)* Mary—

MARY: Who's playing the god damn piano, George? If you're not.

*(No one knows what to say, then hearing herself:)*

MARY: *(To herself)* Shit. Fuck...

HANNAH: Mary...?

GEORGE: *(Confused)* Mom. Mom's playing. *(To HANNAH)* What...?

HANNAH: *(Explaining)* She thought it was Thomas. She's been doing that.

MARY: *(To HANNAH)* He used to play this piece to me... *(Then to herself)* Shit... Shit...

*(No one knows what to say.)*

GEORGE: The opera singer wants to come over and take a look at the piano. She's on her way into Rhinebeck anyway. What do I tell her? I'll tell her she can come. *(Going out)* She asked if it's really a Bechstein...

*(Piano music continues off.)*

HANNAH: Upright... Bechstein *upright.* There's a big price difference we learned. But it'll help. *(To MARY)* The singer's eager. *(To JOYCE)* Our sign's been up at Bard for like two days...

MARY: *(Trying to explain)* It's going through the boxes, Hannah...

HANNAH: I know. I know...

MARY: Each one you open and it's like...

HANNAH: I know. I see that.

*(Then)*

JOYCE: *(Trying to make a joke)* I should go and say, 'Mom is that how you're going to play it? Is that how you're going to play it.'

KARIN: *(With some of Thomas' notebooks)* Mary, when I'd go and see one of Thomas' plays, I'd always think: 'is that me up there on the stage? Is that character me?' Did you do that too?

MARY: I don't know.

HANNAH: You told me you did.

KARIN: 'That character so sounds like me. Like something I'd say'... Of course it was in a completely different context—in a play. Spoken by a character... *(She puts a notebook back, and will take out another.)*

*(GEORGE enters.)*

GEORGE: She'll be here in a little while. She 'wants to see what we got.' 'It's a Bechstein...'

HANNAH: Your mother coming back?

*(Off, PATRICIA plays the Bach.)*

GEORGE: *(Shrugs)* Let's leave her alone...

JOYCE: *(Listening)* We all played this. We all learned to play this...

*(They listen.)*

GEORGE: Yeh...

*(Then)*

KARIN: *(Another book)* Thomas gave me a copy of this... When I visited last fall... When Mary so generously invited me up here...

MARY: He asked me to ask you...

KARIN: Thomas hardly could speak... He had a pile of these on his desk in his bedroom. He gave me one. Why did he have so many copies, Mary?

MARY: He was always talking about adapting it into a play.

OTHERS: A play. Theater.

MARY: He was always trying to get someone to pay him to do that.

HANNAH: What's the book?

KARIN: I love the title: *Wandering Star*. Sholom Aleichem.

GEORGE: I don't know it.

KARIN: I've read it now twice...

GEORGE: He wanted to make it into a play? What's it about? Let me see... *(Takes the book)*

KARIN: Two young people, a boy and a girl. They live in a 'Shtetl'; over a hundred years ago. They're Jewish. Their families have plans for them. But the kids are in love. One day a theater company—

JOYCE: *(To MARY)* I knew there had to be a theater somewhere—

*(Music off stops.)*

KARIN: *(Over this)*—of Yiddish actors, singers, comes to town. The kids run away with these actors, but it just so happens that this theater group is fighting amongst itself and so it splits, one half goes off in one direction, the other in another... The boy goes off with one, the girl with the other. They are separated. Right at the point when they thought—they'd be together forever... Years pass. One is in Germany, the other in Paris, then London; they write letters that never get delivered, their paths never cross. He becomes a star actor; she a great singer. More years go by, until at the peak of their fame, they each learn the other is in New York City. They plan to meet. They meet—at the zoo. Nice touch....

*(They notice the piano music start up.)*

KARIN: Each now has married, each has children, they have and have had lovers. They both know, without

saying anything, that it's too late for them now. The
end. *(Then)* As I was reading the story, you can tell me
if you think I'm imagining this, I can imagine things—

HANNAH: *(To* GEORGE*)* May I see?

KARIN: —this book's a celebration of searching for each
other; *and* their forgetting each other; a celebration of
both their faithfulness *and* their faithlessness. Of their
just being human…

MARY: Was he able to write anything in your copy,
Karin?

KARIN: No. Nothing…

*(Then)*

JOYCE: Remember when Thomas all of a sudden
decided he was Jewish?

GEORGE: Oh god. Don't remind me.

JOYCE: It really bothered you. 'George, I think we're
Jewish. I've done the research!' You never knew where
he was going next.

HANNAH: *(Defending Thomas)* He was searching—.

JOYCE: For what?? 'Thomas, what the hell are you
talking about?'

MARY: *(To* GEORGE*)* You got really upset. Why did that
upset you?

GEORGE: *('I'm not the only one:')* Joyce got upset.

JOYCE: He's telling us what we are… He'd just go off
half-cocked.

GEORGE: He could just dream things up.

HANNAH: He was a writer.

GEORGE: We're not Jewish.

JOYCE: *(Over this)* No.

MARY: He was only trying to figure something out—

GEORGE: What? Figure out what? He was just being—
(*To* HANNAH) you know what I mean?

HANNAH: I don't. What?

GEORGE: Romantic.

JOYCE: He's right. You're right.

HANNAH: (*Over this*) Being Jewish is romantic??

GEORGE: That's not what I'm saying.

HANNAH: (*Over this*) Try telling that to someone whose family—.

GEORGE: He needed to feel *different*. That's what I'm saying. There's nothing wrong with being Jewish. Come on. (*Mocking, as Thomas*) 'What am I?' 'Who am I?' I really disliked that side of Thomas...

JOYCE: Me too. To be honest.

MARY: (*Trying to explain*) The way he explained it to me...

(*Off* PATRICIA *has stopped playing; no one notices.*)

GEORGE: Do we have to talk about this?

HANNAH: Let Mary talk—.

GEORGE: Joyce?

MARY: He said—he just couldn't understand where all this—the importance that your father and your mother placed on—on being cultured. Where had *that* come from? That's what he was asking.

GEORGE: 'Jewish people' want to give their kids culture and education. I know, Mary. But that's such a cliché. It's a cliché!

KARIN: I don't know about this.

MARY: Your relatives were farmers.

GEORGE: Why can't farmers—?

HANNAH: Isn't there some truth—?

GEORGE: I have friends who are farmers. They read!

MARY: Thomas wasn't putting down farmers.

GEORGE: I think he was. I live in the country.

HANNAH: So do I.

GEORGE: Well, that's how I took it.

MARY: George, I'm just saying I think Thomas was trying to figure out why he felt so different. Is there something wrong with that?

GEORGE: With feeling that? No. But what about telling us all what *we* should feel or think? Who *we* are? He wasn't just talking about himself.

MARY: Your grandpa was a mechanic for rich people's cars. *(To* KARIN*)* Did Thomas ever tell you that?

KARIN: No.

MARY: I guess he only talked about that later…

GEORGE: He was ashamed.

MARY: I don't think so. Maybe. Maybe he was. But then he wasn't. And your Grandmother—she was a maid.

HANNAH: For the Astors… Just down the road here.

MARY: *(Over this)* And your father was given piano lessons—at something like—.

JOYCE: No more than five years old.

MARY: Your grandparents didn't play. *And* the fiddle. Your father played the fiddle. Thomas only wanted to know where that came from. Where the hell he came from.

GEORGE: Mary—

HANNAH: Let her talk.

MARY: *(Another point)* At the Jewish Museum in Manhattan—. Hannah, I don't think we ever told you this. Thomas and I were there once: and came across a plaque, I think it comes from Austria—

JOYCE: *(To* KARIN*)* Our relatives came from there.

MARY: —listing Jewish soldiers from one village who had died in World War One. One name: Gabrielski.

GEORGE: What does that—?

MARY: I know that proves nothing. Thomas knew that.

KARIN: *(Trying to keep up, over this)* This is all new to me. Where in Austria?

JOYCE: Thomas dragged Mary to the 'ancestral' village.

MARY: *(Over the end of this)* That was wife number two, Joyce. This was before me. I didn't go. *(To* KARIN*)* They made her wear a dirndl, Karin. I saw a picture... *(Smiles, then to* GEORGE*)* 'Where do I come from?' 'Where do I fit in?' 'Each day, why do I feel more and more different?' *(Then)* I don't think that deserves to be mocked...

JOYCE: I don't think George is mocking the questioning, Mary. *(To* GEORGE*)* Are you?

GEORGE: No.

JOYCE: It's the being told what the answers are, Mary. Our big brother was always telling us what to do. What everyone had to read. What we had to read. What T V show— 'Quick, turn on channel...'

MARY: Thomas got excited about things. He wanted to share. For me that was a good thing.

JOYCE: *(Over)* What hot actor to watch out for.

GEORGE: Who we 'had' to vote for—.

MARY: What?

JOYCE: George and I were just talking about this on the phone last week. You probably don't even know this.

GEORGE: 'Obama, George...'

MARY: What are you talking about?

JOYCE: Just one example, Mary.

GEORGE: One day Thomas comes 'home'—

JOYCE: Like eight years ago. So he's not sick yet. I don't think you were here with him.

GEORGE: And, we're here in this kitchen. Joyce is visiting too. And Thomas tells us 'we gotta vote for Hillary.' The first woman blah blah blah.

JOYCE: 'It's so exciting.'

MARY: I remember him saying that.

GEORGE: *(Over this)* 'I've heard her speak in person.' He gets us excited.

JOYCE: Mom starts shouting: 'Where's the bell? Get out the bell.'

KARIN: *(Over this)* What? I don't understand.

JOYCE: Where is the bell?

HANNAH: *(Over this)* When the Gabriels start talking politics, Karin—.

JOYCE: Mom has this little bell you can ring bell for—

HANNAH: For 'time out.'

JOYCE: Mary, where is it? It used to be in the kitchen.

MARY: It broke. The little clang-er broke.

HANNAH: During the conventions.

MARY: We had to throw it out, Joyce.

GEORGE: Anyway, two months later—Thomas is on the phone: *(Excited voice)* 'Forget Hillary, it's Obama! Oh my god have you been watching this guy? His

speeches...' 'What about Hillary—? I ask. 'No, don't be
stupid, George. Obama: the first black blah blah blah. I
thought I'd never live to see the day.'

Mary    I don't see why it's wrong, George, to keep
asking: who you are. Can't he ask that?

GEORGE: Well, he's not here to ask anymore, Mary.

*(Then)*

MARY: No. No. He isn't.

*(Door bell off.)*

MARY: And thank you for reminding us, George. *(She
starts to stand:)* That's the singer...

JOYCE: That was quick.

HANNAH: *(To* GEORGE*)* Shouldn't you be the one—?

MARY: *(Wiping her hands)* I'll go. I'll get it before
Patricia scares them off... *(She starts to go.)*

JOYCE: Don't let her do that. Please...

HANNAH: *(Same time)* George, go... Go... Let George,
Mary. Please.

*(This stops* MARY. GEORGE *gets up.)*

HANNAH: Remember you like people to like you.
That's not good....

*(As* GEORGE *goes)*

HANNAH: Don't give it away... He's getting tougher.
*(To* MARY*)* He'll do fine...

*(Short pause)*

JOYCE: She came right away. She must be interested.

MARY: Must be.

HANNAH: Probably coming into the village anyway.
Sounded like that. She's just checking it out...

MARY: Patricia going to stay in there...?

(HANNAH *shrugs.*)

MARY: 'Where do we fit in?' 'Where do we belong?' Thomas was just asking that. 'Why do I feel like a stranger in my own country?'

JOYCE: I remember Thomas saying that right here at this kitchen table. I think I know what he meant.

MARY: (HANNAH) You sure you don't want to be in there with him?

HANNAH: He's fine. I think he's going to be fine.

JOYCE: Think what Thomas would be feeling now, Mary...

MARY: Oh god. I don't even want to think about that. So maybe it's for the best, Joyce...

HANNAH: Mary, this morning—I think Thomas would have liked this. His warped sense of humor.

MARY: What? It wasn't that 'warped'—.

HANNAH: George was talking to one of the weekenders that he does work for. A Democrat. When did the rich people become Democrats?

KARIN: I don't know.

HANNAH: How did that happen?

MARY: It just did.

HANNAH: For some reason George tells the guy about his Mom and his problems. The mortgage. I don't know what he was expecting. But this guy just looks at George, looks him up and down, at his jeans that are stained, his dirty hands, and says 'I hope George you're now not going to vote for— 'him'.'

JOYCE: You're kidding.

KARIN: (*Same time*) Trump?

HANNAH: That's what he said. George was just looking for a little sympathy. That's what he got instead…

JOYCE: People are scared. Everyone I know is scared.

MARY: So what did George say back?

HANNAH: The guy hadn't paid him yet. So nothing….

*(Off, someone is playing various riffs or scales on the piano.)*

JOYCE: She's trying it out.

*(As they listen)*

JOYCE: It sounds good.

MARY: George got it tuned today.

JOYCE: Hannah said.

*(Then)*

HANNAH: I wish I could just talk with him right now, Mary.

MARY: Thomas? Me too. He'd just let me rant. He always just let me rant…. Now you just find yourself ranting along with everybody else and no one's listening. Thomas listened.

HANNAH: There's no news anymore, what happened to news? It's all screaming. It has just fucked up everything. Everybody I know seems fucked up by it. I'd like to talk about that with Thomas.

KARIN: The election?

HANNAH: *(Over this)* And it just makes me feel dirty, Mary.

MARY: I understand that.

HANNAH: Filthy. Like you just want to shower it off. That's what I feel.

MARY: 'Who are we?' I think we all should be asking that. *(Repeats)* `Where do we belong?' `Is this really our country?' Thomas was always asking that too.

*(Then)*

JOYCE: When I was serving the billionaires last night— you know, that's why my boss wanted us there, just to serve. I'd stand right next to some rich person, holding my tray. They don't look at you.

HANNAH: That's the job, Joyce. Welcome to my life.

JOYCE: And I overhear a woman say and this is a quote: 'These days, Tony, I'm only reading things that I agree with.'

MARY: Oh listen, I hear Thomas laughing...

*(Scales have stopped.)*

JOYCE: Maybe they're talking business.

*(Scales start again.)*

JOYCE: No...

KARIN: There's a teacher at my school who says she's pulled out the cable from her T V. Just yanked it out and used pliers to snap off that little metal pin inside. She did that, she said, in case she ever got tempted again.

JOYCE: Soon they debate. We should watch that. Shouldn't we? The debate?

*(They think about this, then:)*

HANNAH: 'Hillary, please be human.' Please.

JOYCE: *He* won't be human.

MARY: She's not— *(Human)*?

HANNAH: Paulie doesn't think so.

KARIN: Getting sick is human...

HANNAH: And Paulie isn't alone.

*(Then)*

JOYCE: Everyone last night at the party was talking about her 'coming back on the campaign trail.' How `she's looking great'. She's going to be on Jimmy Fallon too. On Monday.

MARY: Too?

JOYCE: He was on last night…

HANNAH: You think she'll be human on Jimmy Fallon?

JOYCE: He wasn't.

HANNAH: He let Fallon rub his hair.

JOYCE: That's now the criteria for being human?

MARY: *(Over the end of this, to* HANNAH*)* You watched Jimmy Fallon?

HANNAH: *(Over this)* I woke up. I couldn't sleep… *(Then)* A friend of mine in the village. She owns a little dress shop.

MARY: I know who you mean.

HANNAH: *(To* JOYCE*)* You don't know her. I don't know how she makes a living. *(To* MARY*)* Do you?

MARY: No.

JOYCE: *(About the piano)* When are they going to talk business…?

MARY: She hasn't left.

HANNAH: *(Continues)* There's nothing fancy in her store. Very basic stuff. Nothing special for the rich weekender—no exotic olive oils—.

MARY: No five dollar pieces of chocolate that are this big *(Very small)*. Five dollars.

HANNAH: No funny kids' t-shirts: 'London. Paris. Rhinebeck.' Just normal, real, human stuff. Anyway, whenever we run into each other now, and I just thought of this—she always says the same thing, and always with a smile: "Hannah," she says, "what about us?"

Thomas used to say that. 'What about us?'

KARIN: Did he?

JOYCE: I can hear his voice. 'What about us?'

MARY: What I hear is him always being hopeful.

JOYCE: What do you mean?

MARY: Thomas was always looking for something hopeful...

JOYCE: Hence—Obama...

MARY: For about five minutes, Joyce. *(To* HANNAH*)*
Anyway that's one thing I remember about my husband.

HANNAH: That's a gift. I wish I had it.

KARIN: Me too.

JOYCE: Me too.

MARY: 'Things will get better, Mary.' 'You'll see, things
get better.' *(Then)* Some days when I was tired, after
a long day, I'd come home and he'd take one look
at me and say: 'Mary, things get better.' I never said
back what I was thinking: 'But Thomas, can't things
sometimes get worse?'

*(Lights fade.)*

# 7.
## What Did You Expect?

*(The same, a short time later)*

*(The women wait.)*

*(Short pause.* JOYCE *washes her hands.)*

(MARY *works on her marinade, then: off, someone has begun to play Bach's aria on the piano.*)

HANNAH: I think that's George, he's showing off to the opera singer. That's not a good sign. You think I should—?

MARY: I do. I really do.

JOYCE: Me too. Go, Hannah. Go. Go... Hurry...

HANNAH: He'll want her to know he's a musician too... (*She hurries off.*)

JOYCE: What are we asking? Did George have it appraised?

MARY: We looked on line. (*Shrugs*) It's an upright. Five thousand? It'll help. Fingers crossed.

JOYCE: Think of all the cans of Coke we spilled on that piano...I nearly broke my ankle on its leg...Thomas was chasing me. (*Another:*) Once, Mary, Thomas climbed up and on it and sang 'Kookie, Kookie Lend Me Your Comb.' Then he fell off. Mom and Dad were out somewhere... They never knew... Dad did the pedals for me, when I started; I sat on his lap. I did the keys, the ones I could reach...

(*Off, the music has stopped. All notice this.*)

MARY: One of the notebooks Karin and I were looking through last night—about a show Thomas was writing... It's about a piano. A player piano. Set in Russia. He loved everything Russian.

JOYCE: Oh he did.

KARIN: I know.

MARY: There's a party and the piano all on its own starts playing tunes everyone knows. How does it do it? How does it know? (*Shrugs*) But there's such a wave of 'comfort' —everyone at the party feels it; being accompanied, I think...

JOYCE: I was driving back from Tanglewood with Thomas. I was really young. He'd taken me to some piano concert. We'd just gotten off the Taconic. And we see, on a parallel road, a house on fire. We see the frame of the house through the flames. Everything else is quiet, but the house is totally engulfed. We stopped and watched for a while. Driving here from Hudson I suddenly remembered that...

(HANNAH *and* PATRICIA *are entering:*)

MARY: Dinner should be ready.

HANNAH: She's gone. George went down a thousand. Karin, will you please find something else to sell? Now!

MARY: Karin, Hannah was joking. We're doing our best.

(KARIN *starts to go back to the boxes.*)

HANNAH: She told him there's a Bechstein upright for sale in Hudson.

JOYCE: She was negotiating...

HANNAH: So he went down a thousand. And she wrote a check... (*This sinks in, then:*) I wonder how much it's really worth... (*To* JOYCE) You okay?

(*Timer goes off.*)

MARY: Dinner's ready...

JOYCE: We heard you playing, Mom. I can't remember the last time I heard you play.

MARY: You all right, Patricia?

JOYCE: (*'Smiling'*) I was going to come in and say, 'Is that how you're going to play it? Is that how you're going to play it?'

PATRICIA: I don't understand, Joyce.

MARY: It's a joke, Patricia.

PATRICIA: I see…

*(Off* GEORGE *is playing Bach's* Goldberg Variation #1. *They notice this.)*

JOYCE: I'll put away the rest of this picnic stuff, Hannah. Put some of it in the fridge?

PATRICIA: *(To* JOYCE*)* She kept pointing out: 'Look at that chip on that leg.' 'Look at that scratch.'

HANNAH: *(Again)* She was negotiating.

JOYCE: We've played on it… We were kids. What do you expect?

MARY: *(To* HANNAH*)* He did okay… Dinner's ready, Patricia.

PATRICIA: What can I do?

MARY: We'll eat in the dining room?

PATRICIA: I hope so.

JOYCE: Where else? *(Handing her the guacamole in the Tupperware)* Here, you can put a top on this, Mom… Be careful. Don't spill it. George worked very hard on that…

MARY: Sometimes when Patricia visits we eat in the living room. The T V's there…

JOYCE: And watch the news? Not while I'm eating. Not now.

MARY: I can't get the story of the house on fire out of my head.

KARIN: I think George did a really nice job with the guacamole. Very nice…

MARY: Doesn't surprise me.

HANNAH: Me neither.

JOYCE: *(Getting the silverware out of the table drawer)* Excuse me, Mom.

*(Off, in mid phrase, the music has suddenly stopped; they notice this.)*

*(Answering* MARY's *look:)*

HANNAH: He's fine...

KARIN: What's George going to give his lessons on, now that the piano's sold?

MARY: He can go to his students' homes. Most of them have keyboards... *(To* HANNAH*)* Right?

HANNAH: We still have 'our crap' piano. That's what he calls it. He can use that with the youngest kids. They don't know the difference.

*(*PATRICIA *is having trouble with the top.)*

HANNAH: Let me help you with that, Patricia...

*(Off from the piano: Bach's* Minuet In G Major. *This stops the others.)*

KARIN: What?

JOYCE: *(Listening intently)* That's pretty much the first thing any of us ever learned to play on the piano, Karin. On that piano. Right, Mom? Dad taught Thomas. Thomas taught George. George taught me...

HANNAH: *(To* MARY*)* Bread and butter?

MARY: There's a new loaf in the pantry... *(About the music)* Thomas once tried to teach me this... He said he can teach anyone to play this... Well he met his match... *(Smiles)*

*(*HANNAH *goes off and gets the bread.)*

MARY: *(To* PATRICIA*)* You're wearing the scarf Joyce bought you in Paris. I recognize it.

PATRICIA: I am.

MARY: That's very thoughtful. I'm sure Joyce appreciates that.

JOYCE: I put it on you. I found it in the bottom of your drawer.

MARY: A scarf from Paris, Patricia. It's nice that you're wearing that. To have that.

HANNAH: *(Returning with the bread, having heard the end of this)* "Paris." I'm lucky if I get to Kingston. Bread Alone?

MARY: Tops Friendly.

JOYCE: What's that?

MARY: They ate up the Rhinebeck Stop 'n Shop.

JOYCE: *(As she picks up)* Oh, Hannah, I just remembered, I meant to tell George....

HANNAH: What?

JOYCE: In Paris —

MARY: *(To* HANNAH*)* 'Paris.'

JOYCE: —near the Place de la Concorde. There's the 'Avenue—Gabriel.' It goes right past our ambassador's residence...I liked that it does. I don't know why.

HANNAH: Maybe we'd belong there.

*(No one knows what to say, then:)*

JOYCE: And another thing I saw in Paris. An advertisement in the Metro: 'Learn Wall Street English.'

HANNAH: What the hell is that?

JOYCE: "Wall Street English." And there was a picture of this guy—screaming. Just screaming. Like this: *(She demonstrates.)* It was really scary...

MARY: *(To* JOYCE*)* At my birthday dinner, Patricia told us about this T V commercial she saw...

JOYCE: What commercial?

MARY: This politician, who was an actor.

KARIN: You said last night he actually was a Senator.

JOYCE: You were at the birthday party?

MARY: It wasn't a party.

KARIN: I was. And he even ran for President.

MARY: You said he had such an honest face, Patricia.

PATRICIA: He had an honest face.

MARY: He was advertising mortgages on T V. "Spend down your home…" That's where she said she got the idea… He had a sexy voice… And an honest face…

KARIN: I can set the table, Mary. Pat, would you like to help me?

PATRICIA: He did have an honest face.

KARIN: I'm sure.

HANNAH: Why don't you take the bread and butter, Patricia? You're not going to get away with doing nothing…

(HANNAH *hands* PATRICIA *the bread and butter.*)

PATRICIA: I want to help.

MARY: She's teasing you. She's trying to be a Gabriel.

KARIN: You can help me, Pat. Mary, tablecloth or placemats?

MARY: Placemats. Tonight's nothing special.

PATRICIA: And you can't stay the night, Joyce?

JOYCE: I can't, Mom…I'm sorry. I can't.

PATRICIA: (*As they go, to* KARIN) You're staying…

KARIN: I am. Pat, I live here now…

(PATRICIA *and* KARIN *go off to the dining room. off, the music stops. They notice.*)

HANNAH: (*To* JOYCE) I can take some picnic stuff to our house.

MARY: There's also a cold cucumber soup. We just had it on Wednesday. Let's bring that out too. George liked it. He stopped.

HANNAH: Then we'll need soup bowls. And soup spoons… *(Then)* I'll go get George… *(As she heads off)* I don't think he thought it would sell so fast… *(She is gone.)*

JOYCE: I'll take in the wine, Mary…

MARY: What about your nice wine?

JOYCE: I think we drank that up. *(She takes a bottle of wine out of the refrigerator.)* I haven't told you this, Mary—what Mom said right in front of her roommate…
Mom said she'd never imagined she'd end up like this. In a room that wasn't her own. And now they even want to kick her out of that. The roommate's right there. I bit my tongue—. You're eighty-two years old, Mom, you spent all your money without telling us-

*(PATRICIA comes from the dining room, unseen by JOYCE.)*

JOYCE: —what the hell did you expect? *(She sees PATRICIA.)*

KARIN: *(Entering from the dining room)* Pat would rather we put on a tablecloth. Okay?

MARY: Whatever she wants. It's her house…

*(KARIN heads off.)*

PATRICIA: What else can I do?

MARY: I think we have it all under control, Patricia.

*(As HANNAH enters)*

JOYCE:  Where's George?

*(GEORGE is behind HANNAH.)*

GEORGE: I'm here.

MARY: *(To PATRICIA)* I'll bet Karin needs help with the tablecloth.

*(PATRICIA heads off to the dining room.)*

JOYCE: I've got the vegetables, Mary... *(To MARY, as she goes)* Did she hear me...?

HANNAH: *(Calls)* Get out the soup bowls, Joyce...

GEORGE: What can I do?

HANNAH: He can take the soup. We had it on Wednesday. *(To GEORGE)* Mary says you liked it...

*(As MARY takes the soup out of the refrigerator)*

MARY: You okay, George?

GEORGE: *(Nods, then:)* And you?

*(MARY nods as she hands GEORGE the soup.)*

HANNAH: Mary said she used to make this same casserole for Thomas every Sunday night too. A Gabriel tradition...

GEORGE: But it's Friday... *(He goes off with the soup.)*

*(HANNAH hesitates.)*

MARY: He did good. He did... *(Then)* Hannah, *(As Thomas:)* "Things get better."

*(MARY smiles. HANNAH starts to go.)*

MARY: I'll be right there...

*(HANNAH is gone.)*

*(MARY looks around the room. She looks at the two boxes of Thomas' stuff. She fusses with the casserole. then:)*

MARY: *(To 'Thomas' what she has said a thousand times before)* 'Thomas, dinner's ready...'

*(MARY hesitates, then as she goes to put away some Tupperware in the refrigerator: music [Lucius' Don't Just Sit There] from the theater speakers.)*

*(She washes her hands, drys them, takes a quick taste of the casserole, and after one more look around the kitchen, she heads off to the dining room to join the others.)*

*(Blackout)*

## END OF PLAY

# NOTE

I consulted and read the following books while writing *What Did You Expect?*: Anne Hollander's *Feeding The Eye*, Edward M Smith's *History of Rhinebeck*, Oliver Sacks' *On The Move*; Joseph E Stiglitz's *The Great Divide*, Matt Taibbi's *The Divide*; Peter Schweizer's *Clinton Cash*, Michael J Sandel's *Public Philosophy*; Edwin Haviland Miller's *Salem Is My Dwelling Place* and *Melville*; James R Mellow's *Nathaniel Hawthorne in His Times*; Peter Brook's Introduction relating to Oliver Sacks in *The Man Who*; *Women in Clothes* (edited by Sheila Heti, Heidi Julavits, Leanne Sharpton). The translations of the fragments of Euripides' Melanippe The Captive are adapted from C Collard, M J Cropp & K H Lee's *Euripides: Selected Fragmentary Plays*, Volume 1.

The play Thomas has supposedly co-translated and which Karin describes is Maurice Maeterlinck's *Interior* (translated by William Archer); the musical Thomas has supposedly co-written is *Unfinished Piece for a Player Piano*, written by me and Peter Golub, and based upon the film of the same name (which is based upon Chekhov's *Platonov*); the fragment from Edith Wharton's unfinished novel, *Beatrice Palmato*, that Karin reads, was first published as an appendix to R W B Lewis' *Edith Wharton: A Biography*.

I am grateful to Robert Marx, Joe Mitchell, Dr Julio Urbina, Lauren Weisenfeld of The Fan Fox & Leslie R

Samuels Foundation for their thorough answers to my questions regarding elder care; and Jocelyn and Evan for their thoughts about this election.

*What Did You Expect?* is a play and a work of fiction, and is not based on any living person or persons.

R N
Rhinebeck

www.ingramcontent.com/pod-product-compliance
Lightning Source LLC
Chambersburg PA
CBHW052154090426
42741CB00010B/2260